Awakened Faith

Learning to Live the Lord's Prayer

Mary Clare Wojcik
Susan Anthony

Copyright © 2014 Mary Clare Wojcik with Susan Anthony
All rights reserved.

ISBN: 1499276001
ISBN 13: 9781499276008
Library of Congress Control Number: 2014907948
CreateSpace Independent Publishing Platform
North Charleston, South Carolina

*For my daughters
Always and forever,
Love, Mom*

Acknowledgments

I would like to thank those who have helped me with this book:
- My earthly teachers who helped me on my path: Susan Anthony, the master storyteller in the book; Norma Pereenbohm; and Norma Simon. What I have learned from them is woven through each chapter of my story and my life.
- Those who assisted me at different points along the way: Tom Hartjes, Jim Roussin, Judy Owen, Judy Ditzler, Gary Varney, Georgia Whitney, Jonathan Landon, and Tony Bigonia.
- My children, who were patient as I sat and wrote.
- My sister, Julie, and my friend, Laura, and everyone else who encouraged me to write and publish *Awakened Faith*.
- My parents, for their love and guidance. To my mother, Rosemary, for encouraging me to become a writer. To my earthly father, Vince, who is now in heaven, for planting the seed that a positive attitude was central to true success in life.
- My angels, guardians, and guides for guarding and guiding me on this journey.

Preface

We must be willing to let go of the life we planned so as to have the life that is waiting for us.
~ Joseph Campbell

My life changed when I posed these questions: "Dear God, is this really what life is all about? What am I missing?" To my surprise, what seemed like a random questions to the universe sparked a series of events that were a spiritual call to awaken.

Awakened Faith is a creative nonfiction book that shares my journey and what I have come to understand as a result of me asking these questions. Each chapter weaves in and out of my personal experiences, using my story and relationship with a spiritual teacher, Susan Anthony, to present concepts and tools to help others who are searching for greater truth.

The book describes how, under Susan's tutelage, I was taken back to my spiritual roots and a prayer I said every night as a child: the Lord's Prayer. It describes how I began to understand that the Lord's Prayer is far more than Jesus's answer to the disciples' request, "Lord, teach us to pray." The prayer is a formula to live by. Hidden within the prayer are the keys to our souls' fulfillment. Yet we must open ourselves to an expanded view of who we are and our place in the universe to be able to unlock the code.

Line by line, the book provides a practical application of the prayer's wisdom to deepen our relationship with the divine. *Awakened Faith* allows us to see ourselves as beings who are offered the opportunity to reevaluate, grow, and expand and not be victims of our circumstances. It equips each of us, as I believe God has, with tools to bring us everything we need to lead happy, abundant, and fulfilling lives. It provides guidance to open our hearts, live from our souls, and work toward realizing life's purpose. It submits that we should all be allowed to be truth seekers on a journey of discovery when something deep down says, "There's more..."

Blending my life story and spiritual teachings, the book investigates the metaphysical meaning behind the Lord's Prayer and guides us to unlock our soul's spiritual power through the lens of the Christ consciousness. Through this approach, the book finds both the unifying thread that weaves spirituality, religious teachings, and science together and a gateway to understanding our deeper connections to the world we live in and the universe as a whole. Each chapter explores a line of the prayer and opens an expanded formula for how to live the Lord's Prayer. Each chapter provides inspiration and guidance that can help us through the most difficult and trying times. What results is a hopeful and inspiring approach to life.

In my research, I found, as with other spiritual texts, there are many translations of the Lord's Prayer. *Awakened Faith* explores the traditional version of the Lord's Prayer, as found in the King James Version of the Bible in an attempt to meet readers' current understanding, but refers to the Aramaic version. The book also uses different terms when referring to God—for example, the divine, I AM, Spirit, and Source. As you read, please frame the information in the term that is familiar and comfortable for you.

I have also changed or omitted many of the names of people in the book with the exception of Susan Anthony, the master storyteller in the book, and Norma Simon, the teacher who started me down my path. These individuals have given me permission to use their names.

For some of you, *Awakened Faith* will be a confirmation of your understanding or suspicions. For others, it may be the link that pulls pieces of information together to create a far greater view than you ever expected. My guess is that if you have picked up this book or it has fallen at your feet, there are answers that lie within these pages for you. My hope is the concepts in this book help you heal anything that keeps you from living with power and purpose, as they have and continue to do for me.

Awakened Faith is not meant to be a definitive work or detailed description of any topic it introduces but rather a work that connects the dots. It helps readers understand the similarities and overlap between Christianity and spirituality. It is a connecting web that provides an explanation of how spiritual concepts come together to awaken greater truth, deepen awareness, and uncover our personal calling. In this book, I explain Jesus was sharing information about the same concepts that have sparked recent conversations about the law of attraction and quantum physics. The book shares the information I have come to understand up to this point, yet every day I am reminded just how much more there really is to learn.

Awakened Faith is the book I was searching for when I started my spiritual journey. I offer it to you. May its wisdom help pull us out of the dark and closer to love.

Bright blessings,
Mary

ASLEEP

1

To realize your true nature, you must wait for the right moment and the right conditions. When the time comes, you are awakened as if from a dream. You understand that what you have found is your own and doesn't come from anywhere outside.
~ Buddhist Sutra

Slumber
Smoke bellowed out of a gaping hole in the side of the skyscraper. Against a backdrop of dark, gray smoke and bright blue sky, people were falling. Storey after storey, they floated toward the earth and their death.

Fear and panic welled up inside me as I observed the scene. I tried to speak, but no words came out. I wanted to help, but there was nothing I could do. I stood watching, a distant, voiceless witness to a horrific scene.

The image faded when I heard my daughter call from her crib, "Momma?"

Back to reality, I opened my eyes, rubbing them wearily, and crawled out of bed. I walked across the hall to my daughter's bedroom. "Good morning, sweetheart," I said, scooping up my daughter and hugging her tightly. She looked up at me with deep brown eyes and then pointed to my stomach. "Baby?" she asked.

"Yes, sweetie," I replied. "Your baby sister will be here in a couple weeks." My daughter was a bright spot in my life, and I was so honored to be her mom. I already felt a deep love for her sister, who we would soon formally meet. *Life is good*, I thought to myself.

By many people's standards, life was good. My husband, Carl, and I had great careers. Carl was a computer programmer, who spent his evenings developing real estate. I had left my job as a writer to be home with our kids and was running a successful marketing business from our home.

We were climbing the ladder of success. We had our lives planned out. We knew the life we wanted for our family, and we were focused on attaining it. Together we had goals to grow our finances, our real estate, and our material possessions. That was the goal of life after all, wasn't it? That was where happiness was found, right—inside your dream house or planted in a new pair of designer heels?

But what may have looked great on the surface often didn't feel fulfilling underneath. I had a deep longing. Something was missing. I was constantly trying to fill that longing, yet nothing I obtained or attained filled the void. New shoes and clothes didn't do it. A new car didn't fill it. The antidepressants my doctor had prescribed didn't magically bring happiness the way they seemed to in the commercials either. But lots of people were where I was; where I was wasn't abnormal at all. Looking around, I saw many others who were working to get ahead, loaded down with debt, and busy, busy, busy. Like Carl and me, they were climbing, and good never seemed good enough.

Then without warning, our climb up the ladder was derailed. Arriving home after work one night, Carl dropped his briefcase on the dining room table and stood watching me as I made dinner. I turned from the stove and looked at him. "I am really starting to feel uncomfortably pregnant. I don't feel like going to my business meeting tonight," I said.

"We have more important things to talk about tonight anyway," he replied. "I lost my job today."

Stunned, I listened as Carl explained that the company he worked for had closed the satellite office he was working out of—just closed it.

The company no longer wanted the location and related expenses on their books. All the employees who worked in the remote office were let go. It didn't matter what their positions were or how well they performed their jobs. It didn't matter that Carl was considered their "corporate ace in the hole," their "go-to guy." He worked in that building, so he was now unemployed.

Our priorities would have to shift. Continuing the climb to a bigger house, nicer cars, and world travel would have to take a backseat to making sure we could continue to feed and house our family. I was going to have to step up my marketing business and become the breadwinner.

A couple weeks later, I gave birth to a beautiful baby girl. Like with the birth of her sister, it was one of the sweetest moments of my life. Daughter number two seemed to be in a hurry to come into this world. She was born as my doctor and my birth coach were running down the hall. Push number one: head out. Push number two: body out. Within no time, a lovely baby girl was lying in my arms. The doctor (who arrived during push number two) looked at us and laughed. "When you want something, you don't mess around."

I savored getting to know this new little person, cuddling and loving her and marveling at her beauty. It was so much fun introducing her to her big sister. I was looking forward to reading her bedtime stories and playing with noisy toys. But because Carl had lost his job, the beautiful moments were abbreviated. It wasn't long after that I was back to work. I was devastated, but there was nothing I could do; there would be no real maternity leave with this baby.

Day after day, I packed my maternal instinct in the back of my car and went off to market my business. I looked at my newborn's precious face, and my heart ached. I needed to be with the baby I had carried inside me. I needed to play with and nurture my happy-go-lucky three-year-old too. Instead, I walked out the door early in the day and worked into the evening. I would leave my husband holding the baby as her older sister waved and blew kisses, giggling and happy.

I felt alone and separate from the world. I was starting to feel disconnected from my kids—and, to be honest, I already felt disconnected from my husband. Though Carl and I had always needed different things from life, the togetherness I craved seemed further and further away.

Carl and I had met at work years before and had had an instant connection. It wasn't long after we met that we started dating and talking about a future together. We were married two years later. Even though there was a spark, we didn't always understand where the other person was coming from. Carl didn't seem interested in sharing in life experiences the way I thought a husband would. From ultrasounds to family gatherings, he just seemed put out when asked to join in. And he couldn't understand why I didn't feel the need to conserve every dime. *We would work on it,* I had thought. We would be happy then. But now…now there seemed so much distance. The life I thought would unfold seemed to fade. And for what?

I started to question the meaning of it all—the hard work, the striving to get ahead only to be treated like you are disposable in the end. Thinking out loud, I muttered, "Dear God, is this really what life is all about? What am I missing?"

It had never dawned on me before that I could ask God questions and really expect answers. It wasn't even intentional, more of a shout out to the universe from a confused and bewildered soul. But it seemed as if God had anticipated my question, and the answers were well on their way.

As summer morphed, the days were not as long, and a cool breeze whispered that fall would soon arrive. We were still trying to figure out the direction life would take for our family. Carl continued to look for work. He had some good leads but no job yet. I continued to work long hours, wishing things could go back to the way they were.

We were both shaken by the shift the loss of Carl's job had caused. What before had seemed like manageable ups and downs in our relationship now polarized. At a time in our lives that should have been filled with Hallmark moments, the stress of keeping it all together created a growing rift between us. Raised voices and lowered moods rocked the foundation of our marriage. Things were said that couldn't be taken back. Trust dissipated, and dissonance grew.

Feeling at a loss to cope, I went to see my doctor. After I explained my situation, the doctor prescribed a second antidepressant and asked me to come back regularly so she could monitor my progress.

I hoped the medication would dull the ache and help ward off my growing anxiety. I opened the bottle on my way out of the office and added another dimension to the fog I found myself in. Dressed for success with a smile glued to my face, I was sure no one would be able to sense the pain in my heart. I went on to the next meeting, the next presentation, and the next sale.

Not long after, Carl got a call from his former employer telling him he had his job back if he wanted it. As Carl told me the news, he looked at me with love in his eyes. He had watched me say good-bye to my babies and go off to work even though my heart ached to be with them. He knew how hard it had been on me to have a brand-new baby at home and be elsewhere. He could see the toll the stress was taking on me, and he knew that things weren't good between us.

Carl explained he had accepted the job back, but he asked for two to three weeks before he would start so that he could send me to Paris to visit my girlfriend and de-stress. "I will watch the girls," he said. "A couple more weeks of not having their mommy around will be OK."

Having studied and lived in France, I always felt at home there. From the food to the people and the scenery, I loved this country. Feeling as if this was exactly what I needed, I graciously accepted the incredible gift.

I had met my friend, Lori, during a summer abroad program. The program had led to scholarships where we both had the opportunity to live and study for a year in France. Lori had found a job in Paris and had decided to stay after her scholarship year. Making France my home didn't seem like the life for me, and I had returned to the States. Distance never seemed to get in the way of our friendship, though. Whenever we saw each other, we were able to pick right back up where we had left off.

I was thankful for the opportunity to visit her and catch up. I was anxious to unwind, sort through everything that had happened, and regroup, so I scrambled to make the arrangements.

The Alarm

I boarded a red-eye at the O'Hare airport in Chicago on September 10, headed for Paris, France. I had scored a first-class ticket with my frequent-flyer miles and was comfy in my reclining seat and airline-provided mask and socks. Settled in for the flight, I soon drifted off. I woke up at one point and looked at the map on the monitor. We were still over the Atlantic. I closed my eyes, hoping to fall back asleep.

Suddenly, I felt a terrible reverberation move through my chest. Though I didn't feel physical or emotional pain, the ugly, disconcerting sensation traveled through me. I looked around. No one else seemed affected. I brushed it off and closed my eyes, hoping to fall back to sleep.

Not long after, it happened again. The sensation was stronger this time, and the reverberation resonated through my entire body. It felt like magnified pain and desperation. Clearly something had gone very wrong. But my surroundings hadn't changed—the people around me still dozed, and the engine of the plane still hummed.

I turned to the man sitting next to me who had also stirred from his slumber and said, "Wow, whatever that was must have been awful!" He looked at me in confusion and brushed me off as a strange intruder to his rest. *Oh my God—he hadn't felt that one either!* Crumpling down in my seat, I was red with embarrassment. I had experienced something apparently no one else around me had.

We landed in Brussels a couple hours later. Anxious to complete the last leg of my trip, I made my way to the gate for my connecting flight and waited. And waited. There were no announcements, and there was no staff around to ask.

I felt like I was in a time warp. I found myself in the terminal surrounded by a group of African men, women, and children who appeared to be traveling together. The group was adorned in native dress, wearing flowing gowns and head wraps in vibrant colors. Many women had babies strapped to their backs with slings. Happy children romped and played, oblivious to the flight delay. The swirling colors and radiant smiles contrasted against the heavy silence that loomed above, dark and foreboding. I sat alone in the middle of the animated group, a silent observer.

After what seemed like an eternity, we were allowed to board for the short flight from Brussels to Paris without an explanation for the delay. We arrived at Charles de Gaulle airport shortly after. Disheveled from the journey and getting my bearings, I watched the brightly dressed group disburse like tie-dye at the gate. The colors slowly blended with a crowd all headed somewhere. My destination—a pillow and a power nap in the 16th arrondissement.

I knew the drill well. Finding my way to Lori's apartment meant taking the train, transferring a couple of times to different subway lines, and arriving after a short walk. As I made my way to Lori's apartment, the bustle of the city I have always loved seemed muffled somehow, almost eerie. The cold, unfeeling reality that required machine guns contrasted with the vibrant joyful community I had left behind at the airport gate. But having spent lots of time in Paris, I was used to the fact that the city has terrorist attack protocols put in place. I wasn't bothered that trashcans were boarded up and military personnel with machine guns guarded buildings and the subway gates. I was so intent on my destination that I didn't question why everyone was allowed to ride the train into the city for free. I thanked the soldiers who let me enter the subway system "sans ticket." It made no sense to me, but I knew there was a pillow waiting for me, and I was not prepared to use my rusty French skills before I regrouped and cleared the fog in my head.

Finally I arrived at Lori's apartment building. The manager met me at the elevator. She rode the elevator with me and let me in to Lori's apartment. I headed straight for the couch. I wanted to rest to alleviate my jet lag and feel a bit refreshed, so I could catch up with Lori when she got home from work. My head hit the pillow and sleep came easily… Pulling me from my dreams, I heard the phone ring. Without thinking, I reached for the old-fashioned dial phone and answered, "Allo?"

Lori's voice exploded hysterically on the other end. "Where have you *been*?"

"I was resting, because I knew we'd be up late talking. What's the matter, Lori?" I responded.

"I didn't know if you were OK!" she said as she started to cry.

"I'm fine; why?" I responded. Her cry turned to a sob. "What is it, Lori?" It took her a minute to compose herself, but finally her tears subsided. There was a dead silence on the line as I waited for her to respond.

"Just, just turn on the TV," she finally managed to say.

I found the remote, clicked the power button, and waited for the picture to come in. The picture started from a point of light in the middle of the screen and expanded out to display the scene. Smoke bellowed out of a gaping hole in the side of the skyscraper. Against a backdrop of dark, gray smoke and bright, blue sky, people were falling.

I tried to speak, but no words would come out. I stood frozen as I watched footage of planes hitting the Twin Towers of the World Trade Center in New York City. The smoke, the fire, and people falling from buildings were just as they had been in my dream. My dream! I had dreamt this very moment months earlier, and now it was really happening! I stood in the middle of Lori's apartment, still holding the phone to my ear, unable to utter a word. I wanted to help, but there was nothing I could do. I watched, a distant, voiceless witness to a horrific scene.

How could it be that I had witnessed this horrible scene before? How could I have seen the images of the planes hitting the towers before it happened? The ugly sensation I felt after the dream was the same reverberation I had felt on the flight to Europe. The panic, fear, and sense of helplessness returned when I realized that not only had I dreamt about this, I had *felt* it happen while I was on the plane traveling to Europe—while it was really happening!

I gasped as I replayed the events in my mind.

"I can't believe this has happened," Lori said starting to cry again. "I have so many friends in New York that could have been in those buildings! I feel helpless. I don't know what to do."

Trying to make sense of it all, I tried to calm her. "Don't worry, Lori...I'm sure your friends are OK. Can you leave work?" I asked, lost in my own thoughts, not knowing if I was helping or not.

"I will be able to leave soon. Everyone is shocked. No one can think of anything else," she replied.

"Let's meet at the apartment at seven, and we can figure out what to do," I said. We exchanged good-byes and hung up.

Pulling myself from the TV, I left the apartment and walked out into the busy Paris streets to sort through the details. The bustle of the city continued around me, and yet it felt like time stood still. I walked along silently, letting the sun warm my face. It was clear that the world would never be the same. Because of technology, the entire world had witnessed horrific acts against thousands of innocent people. Terrorist acts that only seemed to happen elsewhere now became personal. These events highlighted—not as a city or a country, but as a globe—what was wrong with our world.

I realized I would never be the same again either. Somehow I had seen and felt this tragedy before it actually happened. How? And how was I going to explain to anyone that I had witnessed this event before it occurred? Who would believe me if I said I felt the vibration of planes crashing into buildings from that great a distance? I mean really, I could already see my family staring at me in disbelief as I tried to explain this one.

Lori was home when I arrived back at the apartment. We hugged each other warmly. She was devastated, not knowing if her friends and colleagues in New York were OK. We talked about what these events would mean to the free world. There had been no announcement by the US government to explain how they would respond to the attack. Would there be retaliation? Would the rest of the world be able to function normally if there was?

Putting off dinner and catching up, we both dialed into the overwhelmed phone network repeatedly, trying to connect with family and friends.

Finally I got a hold of Carl. "You won't be home for a while, will you?" he asked.

"I don't know," I responded. "I don't know..."

As I hung up the phone, I looked at Lori, and we both burst into tears, grieving for all the people who'd gone to work that day and were now finding their way back to a different, more permanent home. Grieving for the state of the world in which something like this could happen.

Sorting through the emotions, Lori decided she needed to get away for a few days. So we made arrangements to take the train to Germany for the weekend to visit our friend Katherine. I decided to take an earlier train; Lori had to work, so she would join us when she was done.

Stirring

I had gotten to know Katherine when I spent a year studying in the south of France ten years earlier. I had always enjoyed her company and was excited to see her again. Katherine was tall and stately with dark hair and deep brown eyes. She was beautiful and progressive, yet in an earthy, authentic way. Poised and confident, she always seemed to have a sense of direction I hadn't seen in others or felt in myself.

After a lovely trip through the beautiful European countryside, the train arrived in Mannheim, Germany. I scanned the quay and immediately saw Katherine waiting about twenty feet from the train car. As I stepped off the train, I felt an incredible rush of emotion. This sensation was different, though, from the waves of ugliness I felt when the Twin Towers were hit—this time, I felt joy. It was clear that it had emanated from Katherine. It had been ten years since I had last seen her, yet even from more than twenty feet away, I could tell she was somehow very different. She had a light around her that was radiant. I had never seen or experienced anything like it.

We gathered my things and drove into town to find a café. We caught up over German cake and coffee. I searched her eyes, looking for something, anything, that would explain what I had sensed. Sorting through the small talk, I realized the topic wasn't just going to come up. Finally, I found the words and asked.

"You seem so different, Katherine. What has changed?"

"Different? I suppose I am. I had a deep calling to travel to South Africa," Katherine said. "I took a job there and moved in with another German girl who worked for the same company. She was very spiritual and gave me the book, *The Celestine Prophecy*, to read. The book was my introduction to the concept of spirituality, something I had never ever thought of before. It opened the door to a whole new world for me.

"After that, I met a spiritual teacher named Norma Simon at a center for meditation and spirituality. Norma did guided group sessions and they were lovely. Norma led me to other energy classes, books, audios, and a community. It is very clear to me that my path has been laid out for me, and I am grateful that I have managed to walk it," she said.

I was so intrigued. How did those experiences add up to the joy that I felt radiate from her? Why had they made such an impact on her? I needed to know more.

Seeing my interest, Katherine jotted down a list of books for me to read, as well as Norma's mailing address. I tucked them safely away as we set off for Katherine's flat.

The Dawn

Two weeks later, the airports in the United States were once again open, and I flew home on the first European flight into Chicago since the events of 9/11. I was excited to be reunited with my family and start my journey. After an uneventful flight, I found my car and headed toward home. I drove on, listening to the news and the post–9/11 update, still trying to make sense of the terrible tragedy that had happened while I was on the other side of the Atlantic.

From out of nowhere, a beautiful bald eagle landed ahead of me, on the side of the road. I had never been so close to an eagle before. Time seemed to stretch like taffy. As if we were going in slow motion, I was able to take in his every detail. His beautiful, dark brown wings were closed in tight against his body. Random feathers caught in the breeze. His white head turned slowly as I passed. It was an overcast day, and yet light radiated from his eyes as if he was trying to communicate with me somehow. I continued to watch him from my rearview mirror. His gaze seemed to follow me until he was out of sight.

Soon after, I was home again, holding my babies and breathing a sigh of relief. But because of my experiences surrounding 9/11 and my trip, my whole focus shifted. Carl thought I was crazy as I ordered the books that Katherine had recommended and communicated with Norma through handwritten letters and email. It didn't matter—I wanted to make sense of what I had experienced. I had so many questions, and I wanted to understand. Could we really know things before they happened? How was it possible that I had sensed the events from afar? It all seemed so intriguing and had touched me in a way that lifted my spirit.

When the first letter accompanied by a cassette tape arrived from Norma, I poured over the information again and again. Norma talked about opening my *chakras*, the centers of spiritual energy within the body, and helped me understand how to clean them. She talked about spirit guides, animal guides, and where I was headed in life. Each grain of knowledge led me to study something new—universal energy, spiritual principles, and cultural traditions. Each generated curiosity about how it fit into the bigger universal puzzle and into my current understanding of Christianity. Little by little, the door to the spiritual and mystical side of life opened in front of me. I was like a child again, exploring, and I couldn't get enough. I was finding realities I had not understood before, and each new discovery amazed me.

Pouring over the information, I started to realize that my 9/11 experience and my entire trip were about me discovering that God was within me. Looking back, I am not sure how I knew that, but that was the summary statement that fit the experience. I was not sure what that actually meant other than that God was not just somewhere out there looking down on us, but within each of us. This was an expanded view of the spiritual for me; it included light and vibrational energy and the metaphysical.

While I was fascinated, I was a bit uncomfortable with this new information. I had spent my childhood in Catholic school, and no one had ever mentioned that metaphysics were remotely possible or, for that matter, acceptable. Everything that I had been taught up to that point indicated there was a difference between religion and spirituality, and I had to choose. But this felt different. I no longer felt as if I was ordering at a restaurant and deciding between pasta and steak. Instead, I found myself trusting that the Chef created a dish that far surpassed anything listed on the menu.

I have great memories of growing up Catholic. I lovingly recall the sights and smells, rituals and ceremonies. But even as a child, I felt that there were inconsistencies. While, on the surface, I accepted the view

I'd been given, deep down I questioned the contradictions. If God loved me unconditionally, why would He have me burn in hell for all eternity if I messed up? And who was Jesus? What was the Holy Spirit? How do *we* fit into the picture?

Memories of my childhood flooded back as I thought about how the 9/11 experiences fit in with I had learned growing up. I rolled the tape in my head. I was a little girl with a doily pinned to my head. Sitting in the dark-stained pews that led to the altar, I was mesmerized by the sights and sounds of morning mass. I was fascinated, yet fearful, as I watched the nuns in dark robes and habits surveying every row to make sure that each grade-school class was quiet, eyes focused on the altar and not each other.

The priest recounted stories of Jesus's life and the love God has for us, his children. I listened and reflected. How wonderful heaven must be; how beautiful the light of God must look. How wonderful that angels carried his messages to those chosen few; how scared I was that I would make a mess of my life and experience the wrath I had been warned about.

I remember watching the faces of the priests, nuns, and lay people who absorbed every word and every lesson. I wondered how much they really believed in the unconditional love of our Maker. They didn't seem to notice the disconnect between the beautiful stories of pure, unconditional love and those of pain and punishment that evoked fear. Did it make sense that I would surely be absolved if I confessed my sins to a priest? Somehow getting on my knees and saying three Our Fathers and two Hail Marys didn't seem to me like it would compensate for me taking the Tootsie Pop from Joanne's desk. Somehow it seemed as if we were helpless on our own, needing an intermediary to ensure we made it to heaven.

Although that was decades before, those thoughts and ideas were embedded in my perception about how life worked and my role in it. I realized that a big part of my questioning came about because I was now a mom responsible for helping form the moral and spiritual compasses of two little girls. Though I hadn't been to church much lately, I wondered if I should turn to it for guidance in raising my daughters.

Was raising them in this way the best thing for them? Yes, I wanted them to develop a relationship with God. Yes, I wanted them to benefit from the community, but I didn't want my children raised in fear.

My trip to Paris and 9/11 experiences had opened my eyes to see there was more. It made me once again question all the teachings that I had been told were set in stone—ideas I had just accepted as truth without understanding why. And I really wanted to understand why. I no longer wanted to just go through the motions of life, accepting what the world offered as truth. I wanted to understand the foundation on which these ideas were built. I was searching because, like so many, I wanted hope. I wanted peace. I remembered getting off the train and feeling Katherine's energetic embrace from more than twenty feet away. I wanted to embody that spark myself.

So I adopted a new philosophy, one that exists in many spiritual traditions: self-investigation. I dug further, studying universal energy and the law of attraction. I started to open the door to different views on the meaning of life and death, past lives, and the afterlife. I asked God for guidance.

I felt like I was being led as my studies and curiosity crisscrossed religious dogma, spiritual traditions, and new-age philosophies. The irony for me was that the more I studied, the more similarities I saw in symbolism and language and purpose. I was amazed to find that what appears on the surface to be many different schools of thought is all based in the same simplicity and grace. What I had understood to be very different views on the world seemed to hold common themes and the same underlying philosophies.

Whatever name you choose—God, the I AM, Allah—they all point back to the same spiritual light, power, energy, and divine being. Looking at the language, I found references to the same light energy and spiritual power everywhere! Everything I read considered the "otherworldly" sacred. They all talked about having a relationship with a higher power, and they all taught rituals and practices to deepen that relationship.

As I thought about the similarities, I realized, *What does it matter if the angle I see it from is different than anyone else's?* As Gandhi said,

"Religions are different roads converging upon the same point. What does it matter that we take different roads, so long as we reach the same goal?" I was finding that Gandhi's words resonated with me. We all have our own vantage point, and the compass that points us home may read a little differently for each of us, but all compasses point back to the same source. Should we really judge someone because they see truth from another angle or use different words to describe what they understand?

Hitting the Snooze

Back at home, life wasn't so peaceful. My new perception added another layer of tension to an already tenuous situation. I was showing up differently in life and in my marriage. Yes, I still felt that I wanted what Carl wanted in terms of success, but I also wanted to grow and change and find my own unfolding grace. Going back to the way things were no longer felt like enough. But while I was questioning what it meant to be alive, Carl was perfectly content with his understanding of the world and the goals we had set. While I was now standing still, listening, he was off, busy achieving. We weren't on the same page anymore, and we were drifting further apart.

I tried to describe the deep longing I felt. I wanted him to understand what had happened with my 9/11 experiences, even though I only had a few clues myself. Though I couldn't deny my experiences, he was not interested in accepting them or believing me. It hurt. Why would he not trust me? Something in me felt the need to be understood. A voice within me longed to be heard. But no matter what I said, my pleas and explanations fell on deaf ears.

Over the next couple years I continued to read and study and reach out to others with a deeper understanding of spirituality and metaphysics. Carl remained uninterested. Our approach to life was becoming very different, and the wedge between us grew. Trying to bridge the gap between us, we tried going to counseling together. Still we couldn't reach common ground.

In our disconnect, we both made choices that were anything but graceful. Our marriage was falling apart. The picture-perfect life was no longer on the horizon. I was watching my dreams fade, and I was devastated. And, in the end, I made the saddest decision of all—to dissolve the marriage. But to find myself and live my own spiritual truths, I felt I needed the shift. On so many levels, the decision hurt.

It was an ugly divorce. From kids to 401(k)s, everything seemed a topic of battle. We had different ideas about what was fair, and we both shared them loudly. Carl felt the divorce was all my fault. Deep down, I questioned it myself.

Needing to move, I found a condo on an island, a new home that I hoped would be my solace. Our daughters, now five and eight, would split their time between their dad's house and mine.

The condo was in a complex that itself was almost completely surrounded by water. Even though it was right in the middle of town, you couldn't tell. It felt more like a vacation destination than it did a midtown neighborhood.

This island was an oasis. It represented the peace I wanted to feel within. Deep down, I hoped that if I surrounded myself with peace, by osmosis, it would seep in through my pores and settle in the center of my being. Like Thoreau, who said, "I went to the woods because I wished to live deliberately...and see if I could not learn what it had to teach, and not, when I came to die, discover that I had not lived," I went into the woods, both literally and figuratively, to find myself.

Even though I understood the spiritual concepts I had been studying on an intellectual level, I was having a hard time applying them to my life. Instead of facing the fears and showing up differently, I resisted. I threw myself into my business, working long hours, and focusing to create an income stream that would support my daughters. I was still stuck in the pattern, listening to what the world said I should be and have and look like. I was trapped and now facing an industrialized, pasteurized, homogenized world alone. I was still not truly listening to the whispers carried through the leaves on the trees and the gentle waves on the lake that said there was an easier way, a more peaceful way just below the surface.

I was mad at life, feeling as if it had betrayed me...this wasn't what my life was supposed to look like. In addition, I didn't feel good about myself. I was losing my confidence, and, because of it, even with all my efforts, my business wasn't progressing. Instead it was going the other direction. Bills were piling up, and opportunities were dissipating. Now a single mom with a declining income, I felt a new level of stress and vulnerability. Honestly, I was downright scared.

My world was caving in, and everything that I had built was crumbling before my eyes. The fear inside me grew to internal panic as I watched the life—the family, the business, and the community—I had built slip away. Trying to stay afloat, I was now playing round robin with credit cards, and the number in the debt column continued to rise. If this continued, my kids and I would be sleeping in my car.

Never one to just give up, I kept trying to turn things around. I knew the answers lay in the spiritual world I had been given a glimpse of. So I clumsily tried to apply the law of attraction and the power of intention in order to manifest abundance. Each morning, I would set out with the goal to do better and be better. At night, I would lay my head on my pillow and review my progress. Night after night, I was saddened by the realization that I had made the exact same mistakes I had set out to correct.

Life began to feel hopeless. I wanted to fold in on myself. I wanted to hide from the world and deaden the pain. I began to sleep more and more—sometimes sleeping thirty-six hours at a time when the girls were with their dad, trying to escape. My friends would call me and tell me to get out of bed. At one point, I shared that I wasn't sure that my life was worth living anymore. When my friends heard that, they felt I should be admitted—literally. I didn't want to go, but they insisted and checked me into a psych ward.

Stripped of anything sharp or pointy, I was now surrounded by people who had issues of all kinds. I sat and quietly observed, keeping to myself. Interestingly enough, staff and patients alike came and sat with me. Each shared their problems and asked for my advice. I listened, wondering why they would think to ask me. Who was I to help?

Still I didn't think I belonged there. The doctor, who wore a pinstripe suit, drove a souped-up corvette convertible, and came to see me every day, wasn't sure I did either. After three days, the doctor prescribed more meds and released me. My monthly prescriptions now rivaled a mortgage payment. The notes in my chart said I had situational depression and anxiety. I called it heartache and emptiness. The end result was the same, numbing life and burying emotions deeper and deeper.

After I was released, I tried to get back to some semblance of life and attended a business meeting. While the voices at the front of the room were compelling, a picture formed in my mind's eye that pulled me inward. The image was a bird with a long neck, graceful beak, and outstretched wings. I started to doodle it on my page of notes. As I sketched what I saw in my mind's eye, a friend sitting next to me leaned over and said, "Do you know what you just drew?"

"No," I replied.

"That's a phoenix," he said.

Hmmm...a phoenix. The mythical bird that at the end of its life is reduced to smoldering ash, but from which a new, young phoenix is born that lives anew. I could relate—clearly my nosedive was in full progress. But until that moment, I hadn't looked beyond it for the promise of soaring again. The phoenix from that point on became the symbol of my journey and the promise of rising from the ash I saw around me. For a person who normally had life all planned out, the only image I held on the horizon now was a mythical bird. Somehow that was enough.

Lying in bed that night, I was surrounded by my own pain. It felt eerily quiet around me—as if a judgmental world was watching at a distance as I hurdled toward the ash. Empty and overwhelmed, I realized I couldn't heal my life on my own. I rolled out of bed and came to my knees. "God, obviously I don't know what I am doing here," I pleaded. "I could use your help."

Half waiting for the sky to open or a plane to appear with the answer scrolled on a banner behind it, I was still. There was no loud, thunderous answer, only an inner voice that chuckled and simply said, "Slow down, whirlwind." Out loud, I responded, "All right, my way obviously isn't working." Humbly, graciously, I stepped back and let God lead. Reluctantly I let go. I would "let go and let God."

I woke up the next morning with a sense of peace. Finally still, I was better able to receive guidance. I felt called to study universal energy and understand the very thing that had tapped me on the shoulder in the first place. Though I didn't feel that I was supposed to become an energy worker, I needed something or someone to truly explain the "how to" I was missing. I started searching for a teacher.

Over the next few months, I allowed myself to be guided. Teachers appeared in my life. Each teacher had valuable information, a lesson to share, and a new tool for me to put in my tool belt for future use on my journey. Each teacher led to another. Still none of these teachers were the one I was looking for.

Then someone suggested that I talk to a woman named Susan Anthony. When I heard the name, in an instant I knew I needed to meet her.

The dream begins with a teacher who believes in you, who tugs and pushes and leads you to the next plateau, sometimes poking you with a sharp stick called "truth."
~ Dan Rather

Coming into Focus
And so it was that I met this beautiful and mysterious woman, who was an ordained minister and intuitive healer. Susan had moved out of the city to an old farmhouse in the country to escape the chaos of the city and to commune with nature.

It was a dark and gloomy day as I meandered through the countryside looking for Susan's farmhouse. Rain pounded on my windshield. The rhythm of the windshield wipers reminded me to keep my eyes on the road while I was trying to read the directions I had scribbled on a piece of scrap paper. It took an hour for me to reach her house, but finally I arrived at her door.

Susan welcomed me in and led me through her home to a small room at the back where she had a massage table, two chairs, and a small table covered with a red silk cloth and lined with stones. Tarot cards sat in the center of the table. A large piece of hematite, with strange brown streaks meandering through it, sat in the corner.

The rain faded to muted background noise as I sat down across the table from her. We smiled at each other. It seemed as if she was evaluating me as I was evaluating her. Susan is naturally beautiful with long, blond hair and striking sapphire eyes. But that beauty is nothing compared to the light that radiates from within her. Her inner light shines so brightly you could feel her beauty and power from across the room. If it wasn't for her peaceful demeanor, warm and caring voice, and unassuming nature, one might feel dim and lifeless in her presence.

I explained how I had come to find her and how I was trying to better understand who I was and apply what I was learning to my life. "I understand that I am supposed to learn about universal energy. I am starting to understand universal principles and apply them. I am successful in many ways, but I'm not where I want to be and *need* to be now. I'm a hard worker, but as hard as I have tried, I'm not getting anywhere," I said. "Now that I am on my own with two little girls to raise, I need to figure this out. Can you help me?"

Susan patiently listened. When I had finished, she explained, "Mary, you can't find your life path until you understand who you are at your core. You have clouds around you as dark as those creating the rain outside. I can clear them away and help you get back on track. That will help you have more clarity. I wish that I could just transport you through the lessons that will keep you from recreating that fog around you, but you have to understand the reason you got there in the first place.

"I will help you reconnect with the inner voice. Then you can again identify that divine light and energy within you that already has all the answers. Then you will be able to see clearly where you are and understand when you get off track," she said.

"First, you need to find that point of stillness within, so you truly understand who you are—a place far from the noise, interference, and influence of those around you. Second, it will also be important for you to protect your energy, so you don't take on anyone else's energy. We need to keep yours clean so that it grows as you grow."

I was agitated. I felt like I wasn't getting my point across. "You don't understand," I said. "I've been through so much—things I wouldn't wish on anyone. I grasp the concepts of metaphysics and vibrational energy. I've been studying universal principles and trying to practice them, but the principles aren't working for me. I'm not reaching my goals. If you could just explain what I need to do to make them work in my life, that would be great."

She smiled warmly. "Let's just start here."

Then Susan did an energy clearing for me. It was different than any I'd received before. With other clearings, energy workers had started the clearing at my head, but Susan started at my feet. When I asked why, she explained that there are many different forms of energy work and that none are better or worse than the others. "We all receive information differently," she said. "This is how Spirit showed me to do energy clearings. Different doesn't mean wrong."

As I lay on the massage table, Susan opened my energy field. Then placing her hands on my feet, she started to do an energy clearing. She moved energy up through my body and out through my crown chakra, the energy center at the top of the head. She moved the dark energy that surrounded me and cluttered my mind. She remarked from time to time about areas of my body she sensed needed to be healed and spent extra time on those areas. Each time she was spot on, pointing out exactly where I had tightness or pain. Even though I still didn't feel like she really understood what I was asking for, I felt lighter, freer, and happier after she finished the clearing.

My assignment for the week was simple. "First and foremost, breathe!" Susan said. "Shallow breaths leave you blocked. We need to move out any dark energy caused by fear, anxiety, and negativity. As you breathe, visualize peaceful, blue energy coming in through your feet. Let it flow up through your body and exit your crown chakra at the top of your head, like the sprouting of a new seedling growing and spreading its branches out to meet the world.

"We release old, dirty energy by breathing out through our mouth. Let it flow through your body in the same way it does in nature—up through the roots and out toward the sky. It is then released back to the universe to be purified. Out, down, and around. Then you can start again," she explained.

"You will feel itchy as you release the cloud that fogs your clarity. That means the energy is moving. Make sure you drink lots of water and take showers or salt baths to clear it away, so you can keep the energy moving. Remember to state your intention as you are breathing in light, peace, and love. Say, 'I'm releasing fear and anxiety,'" she instructed.

"I really have a hard time staying focused," I explained.

"That's common—especially for people on antidepressants," she said looking into my eyes.

I hadn't said that I was on antidepressants, and yet she knew. I looked down, not wanting to explain how many prescriptions I was now taking in order to cope.

"Be gentle with yourself," she added, reaching out and warmly touching my shoulder. "Just keep bringing your attention back to center when you realize your thoughts have drifted off."

On the ride home, I started doing the breathing exercises, drawing pure, clean energy up and through my core and releasing fear and darkness back to the universe for it to be cleaned for the next passerby. The intention became my mantra: "I'm releasing."

When I was home again, I continued to consciously release the energy that had kept me stuck, swirling in a fog of gray, masking the pure white divine light that pulsed under the turmoil.

My body was tired and itched from the release of clouded energy that fogged my mind and my path and had created walls around my heart. Clouds of fear had blocked my true desires and the path I had chosen for this life before I came to Earth. I took salt bathes and showers to help move it along. I thanked God, my guardians, angels, and guides for helping me with the process.

That was the beginning of a relationship with the teacher who was sent to teach me "how to" have a relationship with God and shine my own light. I had prayed for answers. I wanted to understand what life is really about. Now, because I had posed the question, I was given a chance to see things differently. Everything that had brought me to this point (and to every point since) was God's response to my request.

Over time, Susan bridged the gap between what appeared to be different spiritual and religious approaches. She explained how spiritual understanding blended with and overlapped Christian teachings. In the process, she helped me become grounded and create a solid foundation under myself.

Awakening to Faith
I had come to Susan to study universal energy, and yet I was amazed to find that the language she was using sounded familiar. Though it was blended with spiritual, metaphysical concepts and the vernacular, the foundation took me back to my Christian roots. I had heard these words and phrases before. Over time, I realized that the information she was sharing was the foundation for the prayer Jesus taught his disciples in Matthew 6:9–13 and Luke 11:2–4—the Lord's Prayer.

Growing up, I said this prayer morning and night. I said the prayer as a ritual but without understanding there was a deeper meaning behind it. However, the more I learned, the more I understood that hidden within the prayer are the keys to our souls' fulfillment. Yet we must open ourselves to an expanded view of who we are and our place in the universe to be able to unlock the code.

Under Susan's tutelage, I was gaining a deeper understanding of the concepts behind the Lord's Prayer and a practical application of the prayer's wisdom. Line by line, the prayer became more than just words to memorize and recite, but a formula to live by. Each lesson locked a new piece of internal and eternal puzzle into place until the picture of who we are and who the I Am is started to come into focus.

> *Our Father which art in heaven, Hallowed be thy name.*
> *Thy kingdom come. Thy will be done in earth, as it is in heaven.*
> *Give us this day our daily bread.*
> *And forgive us our trespasses, as we forgive those who trespass against us.*
> *And lead us not into temptation, but deliver us from evil:*
> *For thine is the kingdom, and the power, and the glory, forever.*
> *Amen*

Our Father Which Art in Heaven,
Hallowed Be Thy Name.

2

We are not physical beings having a spiritual experience, but spiritual beings having a physical experience.
~ Pierre Teilhard De Chardin

Getting to Know God and His Spirit

It was summertime, and the journey to Susan's house was like driving through a scenic painting. The country road was lined with beautiful maple trees that leaned in over the road, bowing to the random car that passed. The trees were backlit by the rising sun. In places, the blue of the distant bay peaked through as if to remind passers that it is there—even if it was not always seen. Over the next several months, the road to the farmhouse became familiar to me and brought a sense of anchored peace and anticipation of greater knowledge waiting to be unearthed.

In the beginning, I traveled that road weekly. Susan would clear my energy. Then we would sit and talk. Susan would share her knowledge and help me fill the gaps in my understanding. I felt like I was stepping into the scene from the *Sound of Music* in which Maria teaches the Von Trapp children how to sing. Like the children, I was developing a foundation. But my foundation was not *just* centered in do-re-mi but in the Holy Trinity.

Susan confirmed what I had come to understand: God is eternal light energy, constant and indestructible. God energy is infinite and ever expanding. The energy was never born and never dies. God is everywhere. Everything is God. We too are a part of that one divine energy. We are individualized energetic expressions of the I Am; we are God's children.

God is not just somewhere above us, separate from us, but resides at the core of our being. God's light energy as it flows through us is what many of us call the Holy Spirit (Spirit) or Holy Ghost. That same spiritual force is part of the holy trio we acknowledge and pray to. It is the electrical energy that breathes life into our bodies and the holy spark that brings understanding to our hearts and minds. There is no doubt that the light is there, but up until that point I, like many, had been asleep to it.

The more we develop and grow the light within ourselves, the more others can see and sense it. Spirit's love and light was the energy I had seen and felt shine bright around my friend Katherine. It was the same peace and calmness that radiated brilliantly around Susan and that I *so* wanted to bask in.

Like Katherine, Susan was aware that her light shined brightly, and it seemed to come naturally to her, almost instinctually. As I have come to understand, when we strip everything away, shining brightly is instinctual for all of us, and this is not necessarily new information. The awareness of divine light energy is timeless. Ancient cultures like the American Indians, Aborigines, and Incas understood the dynamics of this energy and worked in harmony with it and their environment. But as our societies "evolved" and became industrialized and commercialized, our instincts faded, and we lost that pure connection. The references to spiritual light energy remain while the understanding of the greater meaning behind them, for many, was lost.

Thomas Merton, a Trappist Monk and influential Catholic writer, said in his book, *Conjectures of a Guilty Bystander*, "As if the sorrows and stupidities of the world could overwhelm me now that I realize what we all are. And if only everybody could realize this! But it cannot be explained. There is no way of telling people they are all walking around shining like the sun." Throughout history, mystics, sages, and saints have understood the nature of our reality and have shared truths about who

God is and who we are. Looking deeper at the language of St. Augustine, St. Germain, Thomas Merton, and others, we find that in fact, everything is energy. Our bodies are energy. The physical space we inhabit is energy. Animals, trees, and mountains all express energy. So do our thoughts, our words, and our actions. In essence, everything is alive.

From rocks and plants to animals and human beings, everything vibrates to a frequency; the amount of energy something emits depends on the amount of life force it produces. A rock vibrates slower than an animal; man-made materials vibrate slower than that which is God made. Spirit energy vibrates faster than our physical world does and has an incredibly high frequency that feels cold when we experience it. And when something vibrates very fast, at a high frequency, it becomes transparent. That is why Spirit energy is lighter and more ethereal and more transparent to the physical eye.

The vibration emitted by each of the multitudinous parts of creation has attributes including a tone, a harmonic interval, a number, and a form. Each vibration correlates to a color. When a ray of sunlight passes through a prism, it refracts into seven colors. In this same way, spiritual light splits into seven major colors, rays, or chakras, in our bodies. Chakras are energy centers within the body that have specific divine qualities. Their whirling wheels of energy range in color from red at the root (base of the spine) to violet dissolving to white at our crown (above the head).

Energy also has gradations from light to dark. The lighter the tone, the more positive the frequency, the higher the vibration; the darker the tone, the more negative the frequency, and the slower the vibration.

Energy within the human body responds to our direction and varies depending on the emotional charge we produce. When we experience positive thoughts that reflect the divine, such as joy and unconditional love, our vibration has a positive charge. When we produce a positive charge, our energy field expands, and we shine brightly. We then vibrate quickly and tend to be happy, at peace, and physically and emotionally healthy.

When we are depressed or sad, our vibration is low. The light is dimmed, and we vibrate slower when we produce a negative emotional charge, such as fear, anger, judgment, guilt, victimhood, or despair. At lower frequencies, we feel separate from God and the world around us. When our vibration is low, we tend to get sick, and diseases can manifest.

In his book, *The Shift: The Revolution in Human Consciousness,* Owen Waters explains that the Buddha spent many years trying to understand spiritual light. The Buddha eventually concluded that the only real power is the light of our Creator and everything else—darkness, evil, and suffering—is illusion. Waters says,

> Physical darkness is the absence of physical light. The darkness itself is not real. It is merely an absence of something that is real. Likewise, spiritual darkness is the absence of spiritual light. Spiritual darkness itself is not real. It is merely an absence of something that is real.
>
> Evil is an illusion because a shadow is not a real thing. Light is the real thing. A shadow is an illusion caused by the absence of light. The only reality, the only real power, is light itself.
>
> Darkness can only exist in hiding from the light. When light shines in, it dissipates the darkness, making it obvious where the real power lies. Evil has no power in itself. It is only a lack of light. The real power is, and always has been, with the light and not with the shadow.

We find a similar message in John 1:5 from the Bible: "The light shines in the darkness, and the darkness cannot overcome it."

Divine light housed in the human body extends beyond our physical selves, radiating out as an energy field. Often referred to as an aura, the divine light we project in our energy field varies in color, intensity, and size depending on our openness and the emotion we are emitting.

We see auras depicted in religious paintings as halos around Jesus, Mary, and other spiritually enlightened souls. But bright, beautiful auras are not just reserved for a chosen few; Susan helped me understand that growing the light within and holding the vibration is the underlying foundation for *every soul's* spiritual development. We are light beings made in God's image meant to become the conduit for the divine light of love.

We are all at different points on that journey. The light is not very developed in some. In others, the light is so strong that it shines through with complete certainty. We may not be aware that it is spiritual power we sense, but we know that there is something there—something magnetic. There is a reason people are attracted to those who shine brightly and want to be a part of what they have found. It is the same energy and greatness they acknowledge and want to express themselves.

We even have everyday terms that describe people who emanate a high vibration. We talk about people who are "vibrant," who "shine," or who "light up a room." We may hear phrases like, "She has an aura of warmth and kindness." We also describe people as charismatic. The word *charisma* is derived from the Latin word *kharisma* meaning "divine gift" or "of the Spirit."

When I'd anchored this understanding, a new set of questions emerged. Though I couldn't help but think that even God must be annoyed with my many questions, ask I did: What other instincts had we as humans lost? How does this knowledge fit with what many of us were taught about the Holy Trinity? If I am a part of the all-knowing, all-loving source of creation, then why do I feel so stressed, so strained, and, at times, plain miserable? If raising my vibration is the purpose of this life, how do I shake the negative feelings that haunt me?

You are a being composed of light, love and intelligence.
These characteristics are the essence of pure energy.
So you are an energetic being.
~ Doreen Virtue

Aspects of Self

Week after week as I returned to Susan's, I would settle into my regular chair. I would listen as she patiently explained the spiritual mysteries of life. As we talked, I began to understand that when we connect and access the inner light, we are in touch with our divine selves. Called by many names—soul, higher self, or superconscious—our divine self is our true essence. Our soul is our spiritual self, employing a human mind and body—not the other way around.

The soul's goal is to raise its vibration by expressing divine qualities like love, peace, harmony, wisdom, joy, goodwill, and generosity as much as possible in this lifetime. The soul is connected to Spirit, the infinite source of wisdom and knowledge. It, therefore, has an expanded awareness and can access greater information beyond our physical world. The soul is aware of what it is to accomplish on its earthly journey and knows how to get there from wherever it currently is. It speaks to us through our heart, and when we listen to its voice, we are guided to our highest potential.

The soul is not the only voice we hear, however. What voice does the soul compete with? The ego. The ego is the part of our mind that is *not* in touch with Spirit. It is our earthly self—our individual personality or how we identify ourselves. It is our left-brain logic and programmed reactions. The ego helps us learn our ABCs and whatever else we need to function in our day-to-day lives. It is also the source of our animal drives, cravings, impulses, and self-centered states. It wants its basic needs to be met, including being loved, fed, and clothed and kept warm, safe, and secure.

The ego is the lens through which we understand the physical world. Its job is to protect our physical body and interact with our surroundings. It has a finite view of our experience. It operates based on information it gathers from the physical reality, measuring and observing through our five physical senses—things we can see, touch, hear, smell, or taste.

On its own, the ego believes itself to be separate from other people and from the objects of its thoughts. Through that perceived separateness, the ego feels independent, safe, and secure and, therefore, acts as our protector. The ego even tries to protect us from our higher self, telling us that we shouldn't listen to our intuition—it tries to "**e**dge **G**od **o**ut."

In the role of protector, the ego operates in the same way a squid does in response to an attack. When the squid senses danger, it releases ink. The ink creates a dark cloud that confuses the attacker and allows the squid to escape. The ego does a very similar thing. When it feels fearful, the ego releases a psychic fog.

Just like sunlight, spiritual light doesn't penetrate the ego's fog. In the same way the squid ink clouds its surroundings, psychic fog clouds our energy field. When surrounded by this fog, we are clouded by illusion. The auric fog masks spiritual light and creates the darkness. It blocks our connection with our higher self and Spirit and divine messages. We feel disconnected and separate from God, nature, and other people. Psychic fog blocks our personal power and the flow of creation. Instead of being led by Spirit, we find ourselves being led by our ego's voice, receiving messages that are fear based and limiting. In this state, we are not able to come from a higher place in our decision making or have access to valuable information about our life's path.

The ego self perpetuates a fog of fear and negative emotions that continue to mask our inner light, even from ourselves. It sabotages our efforts to live a life of faith. When we find ourselves blocked by it, we find we are no longer at peace—not with ourselves or the world around us.

In a perfect world, our higher self would ensure total well-being and health. We would express feelings with a positive emotional charge that vibrate quickly, and our energy would be clean. But we do not live in a perfect world. The ego creates struggle and chaos and darkness in our lives. In addition, we are confronted with a barrage of stressors, all of which cloud our human experience. They include environmental toxins, prescription and recreational drugs, poor dietary choices, and past traumas. They also include electromagnetic stressors, like cell phones and computers.

Though we do not want the ego to direct our lives, it has an important function. It was created by God, and its expression of self in the human body is the sacred space in which we presently dwell. The ego is important—logic is important—but we don't want it to dominate our experience. We want to find balance between our physical needs and spiritual development. We want our higher self to guide our earthly journey, working in harmony with our ego.

The light and peace we all instinctually seek is only separated from us by our own ego-based fears, doubts, and negativity—the veil that separates us. We use energy work to clear the fog so we are able to receive divine messages. Energy work improves and repairs our energy field or the sum total of all that we are as individuals, including our memories, beliefs, experiences, and awareness. This work is the spiritual equivalent of taking a shower. Clearing the fog helps us recenter our lives with an open heart. From this greater vantage point, we see what is true and what is merely masquerading as truth.

Our level of awareness—our conscious experience of ourselves and the world around us—is referred to as our consciousness. The state of our consciousness is determined by which voice we choose to listen to—the ego or higher self. Living on the earth plane is a balancing act between the higher and ego selves, the physical and spiritual worlds. Finding balance between the two is known as an integrated consciousness and helps us achieve our spiritual goals. An integrated consciousness is not dominated by the intellectual but works in conjunction with it.

Higher vibration is achieved when we learn the lessons put in front of us; real power is gained as we work to integrate with our higher selves. We vibrate higher and higher as we master life lessons and open our hearts. We become enlightened, awakening to a profound peace and happiness, an expanded awareness, and a deep understanding of the truth. And when we hold the vibration through a complete experience, we transcend this realm.

The Son
Much of what Susan and I talked about made sense to me and integrated with my current knowledge. Yet, I felt like I was still riding on two different tracks—spirituality and Christianity. The two schools of thought didn't seem to mesh for me; there were holes and inconsistencies in my understanding.

I was still sorting through the information as Susan and I sat down again in her sunroom for one of my regular sessions. It was silent except for a pheasant that called out from the row of apple trees swaying outside. Susan looked out the window as if to acknowledge him and then turned to me and was still, waiting for me to speak. Her calm demeanor was inviting. I found it easy to be open with her about things I didn't yet understand.

I sat staring at the floor, quietly sifting through what we had talked about so far. "I still don't feel as if I grasp completely why we are here," I finally said.

Without hesitation, she answered, "We are here to awaken the Holy Spirit, the Christ consciousness, within us. Life is a vehicle for growth and the evolution of our soul. And if we can find true peace and enlightenment, there is no greater achievement."

"You mean Christ as in Jesus Christ?" I asked.

"That's right. Demonstrating how to achieve Christhood is why God sent Jesus. It is also why he sent Buddha and Krishna and so many others—to show us that living a life of faith is possible. The second coming of Christ is when we will *all* live as Jesus lived, *all* conscious as Jesus was conscious," she said.

"But isn't Jesus the son in the Holy Trinity?" I asked.

"Yes, but so are we—we are all God's sons and daughters. Jesus never intended to be idolized; he never wanted to be held above us so that we could not see that same truth within ourselves," Susan added. "Remember not to put Jesus on a pedestal, Mary. When we do, we don't feel that we can achieve what he did. The truth is that he came here as a man in this human condition and moved himself into a humane being. He dealt with the same pressures and fears the rest of us cope with living on Earth. He came to show us all that we could be as he was and live life as he lived—in the consciousness of the Holy Spirit no matter what the earthly circumstances we face.

"Jesus gave us a whole new way of looking at our Creator," she went on. "Instead of a God that is separate from us, who blesses us when we obey him and punishes us if we disobey him, Jesus taught that the kingdom of God is within us. Like Jesus, we grow to understand spirituality and metaphysical law. We come to know that God is the brilliant light energy. We too are created in God's image; we are spiritual light beings living a human experience," Susan explained.

"Then why we do we call him Jesus Christ?" I asked.

"There is also confusion over the term 'Christ,'" she said. "The words 'Christ' and 'Messiah' both actually mean 'the anointed one,' referring to the ancient practice of anointing high priests and kings with oil when they came into power. Anointing a king was equivalent of crowning him. It says in the Bible that King David was also anointed when he became the king of Israel."

"So," I said, "Although Jesus wasn't a king in an earthly sense, he was spiritually anointed with the Holy Spirit. So what Jesus Christ really means is: Jesus of Nazareth, the person, is one anointed with the Holy Spirit, the Christ consciousness?"

Susan nodded her head in agreement and responded, "In his teachings, Jesus made it very clear that we can meditate, pray, and help others all day long, but until we go within ourselves and remember our truth and take our rightful place as that truth—as the Christed being and the son or daughter of God—we are no closer to raising our vibration, our ascension, than we were before. The only way to ascend the physical is by connecting to the spirit within."

Thinking it through, I realized that one piece of knowledge pulled the Holy Trinity together for me in a way I hadn't understood before. It made sense to me that we would model Jesus's example. Living in Jesus's example, we show reverence to God; through finding our wholeness, we acknowledge his glory. It is why in the Lord's Prayer we say, "Hallowed be thy name." Hāl is the old English word for whole or healthy. The term "hallowed" is derived from hāl and means whole, holy, or a state of completeness or perfection.

I thought about Christmas, a day known to people the world over. It is the day we celebrate the birth of the Christ child. People now talk about the second coming of Christ, but I now understood that the second coming is when we all awaken to the Christ consciousness. If the Christ-life and consciousness is to be lived, first of all, the Christ-child has to be born. But the Christ consciousness is to be born in *each of us*.

That consciousness is the goal of all of us who walk the earth: attaining oneness with God and restoring our individual Christhood—or full realization of our divinity. We are here to remember and acknowledge within ourselves the very essence of his example—our true oneness with God.

Sitting in the sunroom, with the row of swaying apple trees as our backdrop, I realized that Susan's understanding of the divine was not based in a specific religion or spiritual tradition. While she was an ordained minister, her understanding seemed to cross those boundaries into what I understood to be different schools of thought—it blurred the lines of Christianity and Eastern philosophy. It pulled to the forefront Christian terms that before had receded into the background; I vividly remember studying Jesus life while I was in grade school. I don't remember learning much about the Holy Spirit.

"How is it that you have come to understand so much?" I asked.

"My father was an atheist," she responded. "My mother hated God. So as a child, I went to church with other families. I went to every kind of church there was. I realized that I was gathering my truths and that each church had something that vibrated as truth. But fear, hell, and punishment didn't fit—not with the God I knew. Then I studied Buddha, Zen, and Krishna, and I realized I didn't have to choose one.

"When I had questions, I posed them to the universe and waited for answers. I had the faith and knowing that the answers would come. As the information came, I would ask myself, 'Does this vibrate as truth?' 'Do I have other information that fits with it?' I wasn't afraid of the information I was getting, and it was always followed with more information to affirm it."

Susan went on to explain that when she went to study ministry, she realized she already had that base of knowledge. When her teachers asked if she had studied the works of other luminaries or read books they had written, she explained that she hadn't but had tapped into the same information they had. It all came down to asking the questions and being open to the answers that come.

"Often when I explain what I understand to people, they tell me that they always knew there was more; deep down every single soul knows this information, but we are taught not to ask," she said.

This made me wonder why there were so many inconsistencies in the messages we have been told. "Then why is it that we were taught otherwise? If this is truly our goal, then why isn't it explained clearly to all who walk the earth?" I pondered.

"Jesus's stories were recorded on scrolls, papyrus reeds, and tablets," Susan pointed out. "These documents were later translated to create the book we now know as the Bible. The fact is that several different people interpreted the stories. Those interpretations were based in different perceptions of what the original text was saying. For example, in the International version of the Bible, Malachi 2:5 reads: 'My covenant was with him, a covenant of life and peace, and I gave them to him; this called for reverence and he revered me and stood in **awe** of my name.' But Malachi 2:5 in the Kings James Version states: 'My covenant was with him of life and peace; and I gave them to him for the fear wherewith he **feared me, and was afraid** before my name.' There is a big difference between telling someone they should stand in awe of God versus being afraid. These differences lead to a far different relationship with God.

"Beyond that, much of what is taught about spirituality is a very limited view of life. We are taught about what is seen, the physical plane, and not what is unseen, the metaphysical plane. We are taught that the metaphysical applies to a few individuals and not to all of us. We are inundated with partial truths and, in cases, false beliefs about how things work. We are conditioned to see what is true or not true based on collective agreement, and these ideas can be like a virus that is handed down to us during our formative years. They are really byproducts of other people's thinking. People may stay in that mindset for lifetimes, but all it takes is a minute to connect with Spirit and sift through the messages and know what vibrates as truth," she explained.

"Remember, this is not about blind faith," Susan added. "It's about awakened faith. Great doubt is the birthplace and the doorway to great liberation. Hold on loosely and be open to the possibility that there is more. This will keep you fluid and flowing. Be OK with understanding that what you see and perceive is just a small piece of what truly is. Keep asking questions, and be open to the information that comes.

Remember that your ego would have you believe you cannot trust your intuition. Move past that and be open to the experience and ask yourself, 'What if?'

"Tapping into greater knowledge will help you find truths. And truth unclouded by doctrine reminds us that the kingdom of God is and has always been within us. Reconnecting to the consciousness of Christ is the doorway that will lead us home," she said.

As we were finishing our conversation, Susan added, "The Kundalini energy, the spiritual life force that opens us to the process of self awareness, has been activated within you. Now is your opportunity to understand yourself and life in a greater way."

Driving through the countryside after I left the farm that day, I decided to try it. I thought about Jesus and his importance in the world today, wondering what his relationship was to us. I also asked God if Susan's understanding of the Christ consciousness was the basis for truth.

Once I had formally asked the question, information started to surface that demonstrated this wasn't just a point of view Susan held—this information is widely understood. Example after example showed me that the underlying messages in Christianity are closer to other religious and spiritual teachings than we may think and are, in fact, reflective of things beyond what is seen. I remembered learning in catechism when I was young that Jesus had spent years studying in the East. His so-called "lost years" were spent studying in Egypt, Persia, and India, suggesting compatibility between Eastern and Western philosophies. I also came across a book called *Lost Christianity*. In his book, Jacob Needleman describes a conversation he had with "a certain bishop":

> I mentioned to him that in my own academic work as a professor of philosophy and religion I had begun to perceive things in the Bible that I had never dreamed were there. I was beginning to understand that everything I had seen in the Eastern teaching was also contained in Judaism and Christianity, although the language of the Bible was practically impossible to penetrate, because it had become encrusted with familiar associations.

Certainly this is not always the case. What seems impenetrable often makes sense if we shift our perspective from fear to love and include the metaphysical perspective. When we ask for guidance and reflect on the deeper meaning in prayer and meditation, greater truths are often revealed. If we want to be shown if something is true, all we need to do is ask. If we are paying attention, we notice that the answers are always provided.

As students of the divine mysteries, we work to develop the Christ consciousness, learning to handle life lessons in an enlightened manner. None of us will ever *be* Jesus, but we can master the principles he taught. The second coming of Christ occurs when each and every one of us lives as he did, wholeheartedly in the light of the Holy Spirit.

Like a flower opening to greet the day, we unfold. We open our hearts and clear emotional blocks. The less negative emotional charge we hold in our cells, the more open we become. The more open we are, the more we allow Spirit's life energy to freely flow through us and guide us. We awaken to greater awareness, greater truth, and greater spiritual maturity, evolving as souls. The brighter the light of Spirit shines through, the larger our energy field becomes; our energy field can grow large enough and extend far enough that it can encompass the entire globe.

Learning to stay connected allows us to experience our spiritual nature and who we truly are. We came to Earth to have an experience, learn lessons as souls, and not allow darkness and negative emotions to keep us from it. We do this by keeping our heart open and staying connected. In this way, like with the tomato juice advertisements, we avoid having a V8 moment when we get home realizing we missed the whole point.

For each of us as sons and daughters of God, enlightenment, or true understanding, is complete when the blockage of the ego is eliminated and all three levels of consciousness unite—, the Father, son, and Holy Spirit become one. Then we can truly speak the words Jesus himself spoke: "The Father and I are one." Whole, holy, and divinely healthy.

God and His spiritual network are there at our side, cheering our every attempt to grow our light.

Applying the Knowledge
The understanding of the Christ consciousness became the foundation for my spiritual journey. Centered in this knowledge, I was ready to learn more about how to apply this understanding and use spiritual light energy in my day-to-day life. Once I had a basic understanding of how to use these concepts, just like the Von Trapp children did with musical notes, I found a myriad of ways to apply them to enhance my earthly experience. I worked with them to master them so that, like an athlete who goes into a zone when he or she competes, I could go back and use the tools anytime I needed to. Some of the ways I built the bridge follow. Ways I applied this knowledge appear throughout this book.

Communing with God
We make the connection through what Christian and Gnostic traditions describe as communion, or our ability to communicate with the unseen, metaphysical forces of the universe in meditation and prayer. When we are connected, we open a dialogue that deepens our awareness and understanding.

When we meditate, we listen. We become emotionally and physically quiet, finding stillness and experiencing an inner peace that helps us create a line of communication with God. We spark the flow of creation, transforming our understanding and, through that understanding, our lives. This not only helps us take on the next challenge in life, it guides our journey, helping us uncover our truths and understand God's plans for us.

Meditation does not mean just sitting quietly for five or ten minutes. It requires conscious effort to be calm and quiet. If we become distracted, we patiently pull ourselves back to center, grounding ourselves with each breath. And when we find absolute peace, our whole existence becomes an empty vessel. God then fills it with love and light, and we feel creation dawning inside us.

While meditation is the most direct way to experience inner stillness, there are other ways that help us raise our level of awareness, such as yoga and Qi-gong.

Beginner meditation exercises are included in the Appendix A: Meditation Exercises.

Meditation and Prayer
Meditating is sometimes referred to as a form of prayer, but meditation is different than the informal requests, petitions, and ritualistic prayers many of us are accustomed to. Often when we pray, we speak to God. We may feel that we have nothing, and God has everything. In prayer, we ask or petition him for what we want for our lives or the lives of others. But when we meditate, we listen for God's guidance. When we meditate, we open to the oneness that ebbs and flows and whispers and roars and is—just is. We quiet our minds. We observe. We open up to a reality beyond our physical world. While there is a difference between prayer and meditation, there are people whose prayer is so deep that it in itself is a form of meditation.

Both prayer and meditation are deeply personal and have their place; their messages are important components to uncovering our truths and life's path. Both meditation and prayer help us communicate and harness our sacred source. Both help us have a greater understanding of our physical world through consciousness. And as I was finding out, there are often much greater messages behind the ritualistic prayers handed down than we might think. Through their messages, ritualistic prayers can act as our guidance system, transforming our lives and our elevating our experience.

What is your inner knowing telling you?
Learn to stay connected until you too can remember.
- Lou Bougnon

Making the Connection
We begin the process of atonement, or reconciliation with God, by making the connection with him. We heal the separation, becoming "at-one." This is different than saying we are part of him, because he

is everywhere. Connecting is like tuning into a specific radio station, and Spirit acts like a radio signal between God's voice and our listening. That signal is always available to us whether we are accessing it or not.

When we "tune in," we allow God's love energy to flow from our heart and convert the purity of the connection back to a positive vibration that provides knowledge and emotional, physical, and spiritual healing. This allows us to shift in our vibrational frequency and feel more at peace and more connected to God and the world around us. We can start to tap into the sense of unconditional love for ourselves, each other, and mankind as a whole. We can then develop a deeper understanding of the greater picture we are a part of.

Tuning in is very different than concentrating. Concentrating is putting all our focus on something and trying to achieve something through our thoughts. Tuning in, however, means not thinking but rather tapping into or accessing information that is already there. We become one with the information and resonate it.

At times, it might feel easy to create that bridge in consciousness. But if we are having a hard time connecting, it is because the ego is doing its job protecting our higher self; when our ego takes control, the higher self steps back. If we think of the ego like a puppy that tries to guard us, we can tell the ego that it's OK for it to go sit in a corner for a while so that we can connect.

By learning how to find peace and being able to listen, we will receive messages from an inner voice to guide our lives. The voice will send us messages that are positive and encouraging. Sometimes the voice will send us outside our comfort zone, but the voice is never based in fear.

Back in my life, the divorce was further behind us now. My daughters, now seven and ten, and I had developed a routine. The girls loved living at the condo. Together we had fun exploring the island, going for long walks, marveling at the wildlife, and finding small treasures, like pebbles and dandelions and daisies to bring home and enjoy. I continued to explore my relationship with God and his spirit. And I continued my journey of healing with Susan, working to move past what had felt like my own personal hell.

On one of my regular visits to see Susan, we talked about making the connection with God. "When we understand what it feels like to be in our purest, most peaceful state, we can see the world in a new light. When we are in this state of bliss, we can find peace and comfort, even in the most trying of circumstances, and we can go there anytime we need," she explained.

"Yeah," I said, "I grew up thinking I needed to be in church to commune with God, and now I'm learning that every moment, every day, no matter where I am at the time, I have the ability to tune in."

"Jesus didn't use a building to commune with God," she responded. "He went out and stood on a rock. We can have a relationship with God directly and wherever we are. We don't need an intermediary or a building to do that."

Susan shared with me how deeply connected she felt to God when she was in nature. Indeed, Susan was the closest thing to St. Francis of Assisi that I had ever met. Animals seemed to seek her out. Birds especially seemed to interact and have a relationship with her, instead of living side-by-side in the world the way the rest of us seem to. They would often flock near her, sometimes land on her shoulder, and seemed to have conversations with her.

"I didn't have the best childhood," Susan said. "But I often received the message that the most important thing we can do is to keep an open heart. Nature helped me do that. Animals would come to me at the worst and darkest moments and pull the pain. And being in nature, and feeling one with it, helps me understand that you and I are no different than a tree."

I was beginning to understand. The tree is God being a tree. The pheasant was God being a pheasant. The blade of grass was God being a blade of grass. We really were no different. We are all here on Earth having an I Am experience and learning something.

Still I was being the me who I had learned to be. I was struggling to strike that chord of balance between my ego and higher self, and the climb felt painful.

"Don't make it about what happens out here," she said, motioning with her arm to the world around us. "Decide to stay open regardless."

She was right. I needed to look past what the ego-based world said my life should look like. I needed to focus on the light within that had called to me and learn what it had to say.

I realized that with Susan's help, I was experiencing the divine in a new way. I was beginning to understand who *Our Father, which art in heaven* was. I had a reverence for him and for life in a way I hadn't before. With that reverence, I had a deeper experience in which my awareness of the world was expanding.

One day I came across the Aramaic version of the Lord's Prayer. I was amazed as I read a translation of the original prayer. One phrase stood out to me and my jaw dropped: *Radiant One, You shine within us, outside us—even darkness shines—when we remember.* I continue to be in awe each time information comes that solidifies my understanding.

Faith is a knowledge within the heart, beyond the reach of proof. Faith is an oasis in the heart which will never be reached by the caravan of thinking. Doubt is a pain too lonely to know that faith is its twin brother.
~ Khalil Gibran

Absolute Faith

All of these tools are great, but they don't get you very far without having a level of trust and faith. We build our faith until it is absolute. There is more to this than just belief. Absolute faith is the "I know." It is the state of being in which there is not a doubt in our mind. It is that inner certainty that knows absolutely without knowing how it knows.

In faith, we walk a different path. We live in a state of knowing that God is guiding our lives. We know that our requests are heard and our prayers answered. We believe that the desires we hold in our heart will be fulfilled. We trust our awareness.

Awareness is the key to our spiritual growth—developing our awareness we are able to understand the world from a greater and greater vantage point. We trust the information we receive and are open to the messages that we are provided from beyond our physical world. We allow ourselves to let go of all judgments or preconceived notions we have of life and the universe sends us so many signs that affirm our understanding that no one can move us from it.

In *Return to Love, Reflections on the Principles of a Course in Miracles*, the *New York Times* best-selling author, Marianne Williamson says it this way:

> We can let our lives be directed by the same force that makes flowers grow...To trust in the force that moves the universe is faith. Faith isn't blind, it's visionary. Faith is believing that the universe is on our side, and that the universe knows what it's doing.
>
> Faith is a psychological awareness of an unfolding force for good, constantly at work in all dimensions. Our attempts to direct this force only interferes with it. Our willingness to relax into it allows it to work on our behalf.

I was beginning to understand that absolute faith is really an aspect of trust. Yes, I believed there was a God, but to what level was I willing to go with his flow? Yes, I believed in angels and guides, but to what level did I trust that they were there to support me?

Learning to trust is a big lesson. It is pivotal and central to making progress in life. As humans, we want to understand concepts before we anchor them as truth. Considering the vastness of our universe, it makes sense that there are forces in place that we cannot possibly grasp from our vantage point. The spiritual tools we are given work for us in the same way that using a light switch on the wall to light a room does. Even though we don't have the slightest understanding of electricity, we flip a switch, and the light turns on. Having trust and faith and absolute knowing is really the same thing. We open, we trust the messages, and we follow them. We flip the switch that illuminates our path, and we move in the right direction, creating something God would have us create.

I sat on the balcony overlooking the water from my island home, enjoying my coffee one morning. I watched a sandhill crane slowly walk through a marshy area between the island and the mainland. His slow, graceful gait was purposeful. He stopped periodically, standing still and observing his surroundings.

Like the crane, I often found myself stopping to review my progress. I wanted to integrate what I was learning into my day-to-day life, but while I was becoming acquainted with the Holy Trinity, I wasn't even sure who *I* really was anymore. I had let the world outside me dictate my direction and define me. I had been living under my own personal rain cloud, letting my ego drag me through life. Trying to fill the void with people and things had left me empty, numb, and going through the motions. I had been spinning my wheels, working hours upon hours, and creating an energy frenzy that had left me in a nosedive. There was no stillness there. I had not found peace there.

Clouded by auric fog, my ego told me I wasn't smart enough, pretty enough, thin enough, strong enough. I had felt that perfection was the answer, but, in the end, it only left me feeling unworthy. Through all the pain, I had lost my confidence. Through all the striving, I had forgotten what it meant to be me. But there was another voice that was trying to be heard...

Though I now understood the light was there, and shining my light *was* the goal, I wondered how deeply I had buried my light listening to my ego. Surely it was buried under many layers; I myself had built those walls, feeling separate, barricading off hurts, allowing melancholy and sorrow to seep in and become my reality. And for what reason? On many levels, I no longer remembered.

My life was like a disassembled puzzle scattered on the floor. The pieces represented the clutter in my head and the uncertainty about how to reassemble my life and move into something better and brighter. But the treasured light of Spirit that guided me skimmed ahead on my path. On my quest, I continued after it.

I felt a strong message at my core: "let go and trust." So even though I didn't grasp the big picture, I practiced anyway. Even though I couldn't feel the energy, I visualized it and trusted, learning to breathe and move the old energy out and begin to lift the fog. Each layer that was removed became a foothold for greater trust and greater understanding. When

I was paying attention, I witnessed miraculous things that reinforced my faith.

Angel of God, my guardian dear, to whom God's love commits me here, ever this day, be at my side to light and guard, to rule and guide.
~ Traditional Roman Catholic prayer

Our Spiritual Network

When I was little, my dad used to sit on the edge of my bed at night before I went to sleep. I distinctly remember the sound of his voice as he would start to pray, "Angel of God, my guardian dear..." His voice would trail off, and then I would finish the prayer. We said the prayer in English, and then he would recite it in Polish for me.

Though I hadn't realized it at the time, my dad was helping me reach out to the unseen forces that are sent to help us on our earthly journey. Because of this, from my childhood on, I was aware that there were angels. But it wasn't until I started to do deep spiritual work that I understood that angels are just one group of celestial beings supporting our path.

Beyond angels, archangels, and guardian angels of light, there are other spiritual helpers, including masters and spirit guides. They are sent to protect us and guide us through everything from building healthy relationships to attaining career goals to experiencing spiritual growth. In fact, the more we acknowledge and work with them, the more we notice the messages they send us to remind us that they are there and ready to help us.

Angels

Angels work closely with God and humans, and each of us is assigned angels that come with us when we are born. We may also acquire other angels as we develop a need for them during our lives.

When we are in need, angels help, encourage, and comfort us. They may come to deliver important messages or to facilitate some specific healing. They also provide inspiration in the form of ideas for certain projects we may be here to complete. They are our protectors, the ones who warn us when we are being foolish or naïve. They are the beings who provide us information like, "The guy driving in the next lane is coming over, watch out." We can call on angels to guide and protect us. We can visualize them surrounding our home, our car, our loved ones, and ourselves.

From the time I was a child, I felt that angels were protecting me. I even felt as if they had saved my life once. I grew up in a small Wisconsin town that intersected two highways. At the time, the town itself was so small that there weren't any stoplights.

The summer I turned seven, my mother decided I was old enough to bike to swimming lessons with my best friend without parental supervision, even though it meant crossing one of the highways in town.

I was so excited to be trusted with this new privilege! The first day of lessons, I sprang out of bed, threw on my swimsuit, and rode my bike to my friend Melanie's house to pick her up. I stood in Melanie's front doorway, proudly waiting as her mom hugged her good-bye. As we turned to leave, her mother said, "Remember to look left and then right and then left before you cross the highway."

Melanie nodded her head and assured her mom she would. I hadn't heard these instructions before, but it sounded important, so I would do it too.

We made it to swimming lessons without a problem. Afterward, we headed toward home. We rode our bikes to the highway and stopped before crossing. I remembered what Melanie's mom had said. So I looked left, then right, then left, oblivious to why I was doing it. I then set off. But instead of arriving safely on the other side, my bike bounced off the front tire of a moving semitruck. I landed a couple feet back, dazed and confused. In my obedience, I had followed what I understood to be the rules, but I was unaware of what the rules were really there for.

The truck driver was frantic. When my parents found out, they were too. But I didn't even remember the impact of hitting the truck. All I could remember was feeling as if I had been picked up and set down a few feet back. I realized that my guardian angel must have intervened, and I had experienced my first miracle. Who bounces off the tire of a moving semi?

This was the first sign I can remember that hinted that there is more to life than we can see with the physical eye and hear with the physical ear. The signs of the unseen, metaphysical part of our world were there, but I had allowed them to melt into the landscape of my life, because I was listening to other voices that told me another version of what was real and what was true.

Through Susan's guidance, I gained a better understanding of our spiritual support structure. Working toward absolute faith, I practiced differently now. It became a habit to visualize angels by the foot of each family member's bed and by the doors of the house. I surrounded my children with angels as I watched them walk to the bus stop in the morning. When I drove, angels flanked my car. The images were almost comical—angel wings flapping in the breeze and surfing the wind as I drove. It seems that angels have a great sense of humor.

Spirit Guides

Spirit guides are typically souls who have incarnated on Earth many times and have reached a highly enlightened stage of development. Because they have walked in our shoes, they understand what we are going through. They understand the challenges we face in life and are compassionate and nonjudgmental.

Our guides don't come with us at birth—they come in a little later. They know who we are and why we came here. They work closely with us on the earth plane to help us understand our life's purpose, give us direction, and empower our souls. Our spirit guides provide us with information when we ask for it. They also bring us experiences that help us release old patterns and old ways of seeing the world. The life lessons they set up help us to untangle ourselves from thoughts and fears that hold our energy hostage, keep us in a holding pattern, and prevent us from moving forward on our spiritual path.

As Ainslie MacLeod explains in his book, *The Instruction, Living the Life Your Soul Intended*:

> If [guides] have one purpose, it is to empower you. An old Chinese proverb says, "Give a man a fish and he will eat for a day. Teach a man to fish and he will eat for a lifetime."...Guides want to teach you to fish.

Most of us have several spiritual guides assigned to us. Some come in and stay with us through one lifetime, and some will be with us through many lifetimes. Other guides may stay with us until we have completed a lesson or until we don't need help with that particular issue anymore.

Guides accompany us, but they cannot interfere with our free will, and if we want their help, we must ask for it. In addition, guides cannot hear our thoughts unless we give them permission. Giving permission is as simple as telling them it is OK to listen to our thoughts.

At the time, I didn't know it, but I would soon meet one of my guides and understand how he had been guiding me back to myself since my 9/11 experience.

Masters

Master healers, master teachers, or ascended masters are spiritual teachers and healers who have incarnated many times and transcended the need to incarnate further as humans. They are highly evolved souls who have ascended from the physical body but remain on Earth in an etheric form to help us ascend as they did. They support, heal, uplift, protect, and guide us individually and collectively as mankind.

Master teachers will help us cope with our earthly lives as long as we ask with an open, sincere heart and do not intend to harm others. We don't need to ask for them by name. We need merely pray that a master teacher come to our aid and answer our petition.

Throughout the history of the world, master teachers have come to help guide humanity. Many are well-known saints, sages, and prophets we recognize by name. They include Moses, St. Germain, Mary Magdalene, and Jesus's mother, Mary, in the west; the Buddha, Quan-Yin, and Confucious in the east. The master of all master teachers is Jesus.

Giving Thanks and Asking for Protection

I had been meeting with Susan every week over the course of the summer. The blurry picture was starting to come into focus, and I could feel God as a force in my life. That force was energizing and, at the same time, peaceful. As time went on, I started to feel the boundaries of my energy as it radiated outward. That level of energy became easier to hold and get back to, even when I felt tossed about by a broken world.

But like the space between the rungs of a ladder, there were still many gaps in my upward climb where I tried to face life alone, ego intact. In those times, it wouldn't take long until something threw me off again—cranky kids, stress from work, or an argument with my ex-husband. Before I knew it, my ego self was again directing my life, mucking things up and clouding my view.

Seeing me try to hold my vibration, Susan shared with me the importance of protecting our energy. Not only do we create positive and negative energy, we can sense and take on the vibration emanating from someone else—others can "make our day" or "suck us dry."

Negativity in any form can be damaging to our auric field. To keep our energy clean, we ask our angels to protect us. It's important to turn this practice into a ritual, something we do when we get up in the morning and before we go to bed at night. It's also important to ask for protection when we are asking for guidance or going into a meditative state to make sure our information is pure. In addition, we should remember to give thanks to those who are coming to our aid.

There are many prayers for protection, but I find that the simpler the prayers are, the more apt we are to use them regularly. Asking for angel protection for myself, I pray:

Angels to my left, angels to my right. Angels above me, angels below me. Angels in front of me, angels behind me. Powerful angel energy, surround and protect me.

Another prayer that I use incorporates intentions discussed in this chapter. As I say it out loud or in my head, I picture a tube of bright white glowing light surrounding me. I see it as a solid barrier of protection that negativity cannot cross. (You can also try visualizing a clear bubble around you that negativity and darkness cannot penetrate.)

> *To the masters of love and light, teachers and healers, whose intent it is to further the Christ consciousness on this plane, I ask that you surround me with God's powerful shield of white light energy and love—energy that protects me against darkness, fear, or negativity that may be around me or be sent my way. Amen*

Asking our guides and angels to help protect us is a big part of what they are there for. We can ask for their protection on a daily basis for general purposes, or we can ask when we have an immediate need for protection. It is important to be respectful and show gratitude when we request—not demand—their assistance. They help us because they want to; they are not our servants.

I have developed a personal ritual I start and end each day with. I begin by praying for protection for my children, myself, and our paths. I then pray for assistance for other people in my life—my extended family, my friends, and their loved ones. Afterward, I spend ten to thirty minutes meditating and communing with God.

Asking for Guidance

We can also ask our guides to provide us with information and answers to our questions. People use dowsing, tarot cards, astrology, and many different techniques, but it is effective to simply ask and be open to the answer in whatever way it comes. Whichever we choose, we say a prayer that the information be brought from the highest intent.

> *To my angels, guardians, and guides, thank you for your daily vigilance guarding my path and guiding my heart. I ask that you come to my aid, providing positive information to my highest good. Any negative information that may be present, please leave in loving peace. Amen*

Mirrors

We can deflect negativity and help people see what they themselves are creating by visualizing putting up mirrors around us. When we put up mirrors, the energy reflects or boomerangs back to its originator. We don't have to feel it, and they see what they are projecting. We can simply visualize the mirror and state our intention:

> *To my angels, guardians, and guides, I ask that you surround me with mirrors to reflect negativity, darkness, and poor intentions back to their originator and completely away from me.*

Using Light

Susan and I talked often about how to project and use spiritual light. "You will find many people who work with white light, but there are many uses for other colors too. You can use them coupled with a request or intention for information, protection, or a shift in energy. Always protect yourself first and focus on the intent. And remember that we are using these principles for the highest good of all."

Owen Waters discusses using and projecting light in his book, *The Shift: The Revolution in Human Consciousness*:

> If you sense darkness, add light. If you sense pain, add the light of healing energy. If you sense hatred, add the light of love. If you sense despair, add the light of hope and trust in the goodness of that from which we came and that to which we are returning.

I was curious about different colors and how Susan came to know which ones to use for different purposes. The colors Susan shared were not always the same ones I had read were used for a specific purpose. I have come to understand that the colors Susan uses are associated with Archangel Michael and Jesus.

"You will find that different people might use different colors to reach the same goal," Susan clarified. "Remember different is not necessarily wrong. My information comes directly from Source. These are the colors I've been shown and how I am to use them, but others may receive the message differently," she said. For a list of colors and the intentions they are used for, see "Working with Light" included in the Appendix C.

"Remember," Susan added, "first ask for your guides, your angels, or the masters to come in and help you. Clear your space, set your intention, and then project light. Remember to thank them for their help."

The prayer Susan shared with me follows:

I ask that the masters of love and light and the teachers and healers, whose intent it is to further the Christ consciousness on this plane, come and work with me now. I ask for powerful protection around my energy field.

Follow it with an intention, for example,

Please,

> *...Fill me with the loving blue light of peace.*
> *...Focus copper light where I need healing.*
> *...Diffuse negativity in this situation with rose-colored light.*

"The more you work with color, the more examples you will come up with that will help you have a more graceful journey," Susan instructed. "If another color resonates with you, use it. The intention coupled with absolute faith is the important part. I work mostly with aquamarine, because that is the color of peace. Once a person is at peace with themselves and the world around them, other things in their lives start to fall into place," Susan added.

"You can use these colors in other ways too," she explained. "For example, you can put the blue light of peace out in front of you as you go through your day or go on a journey. Put it before you when you set out in your car, go into a meeting, or anytime you shift directions in your life. You can add rose-colored light to your field to create a more harmonious environment. It's important to do it before you are in a situation where someone without consciously knowing it contaminates our field with negative energy.

"It is important to understand that the light needs proper care to maintain it and to keep it growing brighter and stronger as a beacon of truth. It brings you closer to the goal we all have—enlightenment. Then, and only then, do things start to unfold in your mind and the truth that will set you free becomes crystal clear. Your vibration continues to be elevated as you understand, maintain peace in all situations, and share that grace with those around you and throughout the world.

"Also, remember that we cannot project energy onto someone without their consent. However, we can put peaceful or joyful energy out there for people to use if they choose, but the choice to take it in is up to them.

"And on a much greater level, we need to be careful," Susan stressed. "This is not a metaphysical playground. Remember dark energy is very real and is not something we want to mess with. We gather our truths and use them to our and others' highest good and not against them. Karma is a very real universal law, and every action will be met with an equal reaction. Using energy for anything other than our highest good is bad juju," she added.

Being Open to the Experience
Many of us accept the five-sensory life experience as all there is. But when we open ourselves up to having a relationship with God on a different level, a whole new world opens up to us.

At one point I heard a conference speaker explain the process of openness. She talked about people who wear the "I know" badge—the badge that keeps us locked into knowledge we think is complete. If we hold too rigidly to what we think we know, we ignore or avoid evidence of anything that might change our mind. If we do not open ourselves to the possibility that there is more, our awareness or consciousness cannot grow. We block our view of what else there is.

I am continually amazed by the experiences that helped me see how much there still is to learn. The nudges that demonstrate how much greater the picture is and how important it is to have the Zen mind, the beginner's mind, being open to what is possible and what would otherwise seem improbable.

It started, for me, with small things, but there were many events that demonstrated a much grander orchestration of life. And I realized if I held too rigidly to the "facts," I would miss them. Some of the things that occurred were simply small blessings where people showed up in my life at the exact time I needed them. Other times I would hear an inner voice, a voice from my heart, that provided direction. More and more there were signs and synchronicities in nature and in the world around me that helped me see that I was on the right path.

I remembered meeting a woman years before who would talk about a guide she called Bella. Bella would leave her little reminders that she was there, often pennies and dimes in odd places, in between her sheets or on a shelf in her refrigerator. After she shared this information with me, pennies and dimes and even twenty dollar bills started showing up in unexpected places around me. I remember telling the story to a friend who said he wouldn't believe that it was possible unless he was left foreign coins. Sure enough, foreign coins started to appear for him, including a rare Canadian quarter.

The metaphysical aspect of my life has grown from there. I have since had numerous experiences that are hard to pin down to a five-sensory world. Some were beyond any physical explanation. Some might call these things miracles—others might call them magic. I just call them God at work in my life.

I often received information from my guides in the form of dreams. Some messages were cryptic, but others very clear. The more connected I am with Spirit, the more information comes throughout the day as well.

I have had many experiences similar to my 9/11 visions and perceptions that later proved accurate. At times I could see and hear and sense things, sometimes vividly, that were happening in the lives of others. The odds of these things happening by chance were enormously improbable if I looked at them from a purely physical standpoint. Yet, they are highly likely gifts when seen in the greater schema of metaphysical understanding, which so many are now waking up to. Interestingly, I was not scared of the information itself but of how I would be perceived by others, because I had these abilities.

"I was scared to hang my shingle out and profess to the world that I had the gift of sight," Susan told me one day. "I got by my fears, because I was told this was my path. Since I got past the fear of judgment, the gift of sight has provided me with so much joy. I am no longer fazed by those who would see it otherwise, and you shouldn't be either, Mary."

"There is no need to be frightened by what you are experiencing," Susan said. "The Bible tells us that there are those that have been given the gift of prophecy. But nowhere does it say that God would stop talking to people when the book was finished. God has always used different avenues to bring us information, and there are more that you have yet to explore," she explained.

"The fact is that universal knowledge is there for all of us to use so that we can know the divine and live in the light, not in darkness. Seeing and sensing energy is not reserved for a chosen people. Though many people cannot see the light, lots of people recognize that they receive divine information; they just call it something else, like a 'gut feeling.' The reason we call it a gut feeling is because that's where most of our information comes in—our solar plexus. Continue to pay attention, and you will see more and more synchronicities."

Susan was right. I began to notice the patterns, the rhythms, and the meaning and was in awe of the gifts I was being given and eternally grateful for all the information provided. The more aware and open I became, the more I sensed angels and guides around me and the signs that they were guiding me—the gentle tap on the shoulder, a cool sensation on my cheek, and beautiful, colorful orbs appearing out of nowhere. Triple and quadruple numbers appeared too. Often I would find myself looking at the clock at exactly 11:11 a.m. or 1:11 p.m. I'd see triple numbers in license plates, signs, posted phone numbers—everywhere! All of these signs demonstrated that I was aligning with the rhythm of the universe.

Messages came from other people and from nature. I was finding that nature was starting speaking to me the way it did Susan. Cardinals perched on my patio chair while I meditated on the other side of the patio door. Woodpeckers pecked the side of the house in a cadence that was almost synchronized with an important phone conversation.

Eagles flew directly over my head at the very moment I was asking for guidance or a sign. Sometimes the messages warned of danger. Other times, they foretold blessings. But invariably, they reminded me that I am being guided and am never alone. Coincidences? Maybe.

It became more natural to work with and clean my own energy and to project light to create a peaceful journey for my family, others, and myself as we went through life. I became more comfortable using and projecting light and asking for guidance from my angels and guides. I used white light and angels to protect my home and my children and put protection around my car. I put blue light out in front of me as I thought about my day unfolding or went anywhere in my car. Like Susan, I offered peaceful energy to people I passed on the street and people I interacted with. I projected the light of peace to a world in need.

Then I started to see how my world expanded from there and how these experiences helped teach and steer me. Once I was driving in Chicago to spend time with a friend. It was evening and growing dark. Frustrated and feeling lost, I took the next exit. As I pulled over to call my hotel for directions, a large man approached my car. He was heavy set and had an air of coldness about him. I could barely hear him ask if he could help me, because the locks on all four car doors started to go crazy. They locked and unlocked in a strange, frantic rhythm as I tried to get my bearings.

The noise was unnerving, and nothing I did would make them stop. It dawned on me that I was being warned that this was not the sort of neighborhood I should be stopping to ask for directions. As I drove away, the constant clicking of the locks stopped. I drove that car for seventy thousand miles after that, but nothing like that ever happened again.

I remembered working in the kitchen one day when my younger daughter was three years old. I heard voices coming from her room, and when I went in I asked, "Who were you talking to, sweetheart?"

In her sweet toddler voice, she answered, "Grandpa Vince."

That is all well and good—except that her Grandpa Vince had passed away more than fifteen years earlier. My daughter was only three, and

I don't remember ever talking to her about her grandfather. For a long time I had realized that my dad was still part of my life. I was grateful to know that he was a part of hers as well.

One Christmas shortly before my divorce, my ex-husband and I were arguing over who we would buy Christmas presents for that year.

"There is no such thing as Christmas," Carl said.

As he walked away, I mimicked him, repeating the comment, "There is no such thing as Christmas."

As soon as the words left my mouth, I felt someone slap my face. There was no one else in the room, but my face actually stung from the slap. No further explanation necessary there.

In many ways we are shown that our world has unseen metaphysical components. If we open ourselves beyond what we think we know, our life becomes a multidimensional experience that helps our awareness grow as we grow.

Building my relationship with God and his spiritual network, I started to see myself differently. I was more than a body; I was a temple of energy and light—brightly lit chakras, open and flowing meridians, and dancing ribbons of light, like the aurora borealis that illuminates the night sky. The beautiful, blue light of peace flowed through me and radiated outward, touching others on my path. Rose-colored light vibrated around me, pulsing and diffusing discord. A brilliant, white light, like the North Star, guided my path.

Thy Kingdom Come.
Thy Will Be Done
In Earth, as It Is in Heaven.

3

*"Your task...to build a better world," God said. I answered,
"How?...This world is such a large and vast place;
there's nothing I can do." But God, in all his wisdom said,
"Just build a better you."*
~ Paul Ferrini

Finding Peace

I BREATHED IN the deep, earthy smell of autumn. Yellow, orange, and crimson leaves floated toward the ground around me as I stepped onto the farmhouse porch. Approaching Susan's door, I noticed an unusual piece of wood sitting on the porch table. I looked at it curiously. Susan came out to greet me. She handed the piece of wood to me, explaining that she had been digging through a pile of firewood and had noticed it.

The hollowed-out log could have been easily overlooked, yet it seemed clear it was a hidden treasure with a greater message. Weathered and worn by nature, the piece of wood was formed into the shapes of human figures. The figures even had facial features. This simple piece of wood looked remarkably like Michelangelo's *Pietà*. But while Michelangelo's statue portrays Mother Mary holding Jesus, this statue looked as if it was Jesus cradling someone else.

I thought about Michelangelo's work. He had been part of the pre-Renaissance movement. Artists of that period believed that a statue already existed in a rough piece of marble. Pre-Renaissance sculptors chipped away at the stone and were guided to find the masterpiece within. "In every block of marble I see a statue as plain as though it stood before me, shaped and perfect in attitude and action. I have only to hew away the rough walls that imprison the lovely apparition to reveal it to the other eyes as mine see it," Michelangelo had said.

We too are guided to find the masterpiece that lies within. As we chip away at the ego's hold, we find a perfect expression of love—a beautiful work of living, breathing art formed by understanding, sculpted by life lessons, and framed by Spirit's brilliant light energy and love. In God's eyes, we are perfect. No matter where we are on our soul's journey, we are perfect. We will all eventually unearth the complete masterpiece through doing spiritual work, and we can take all the time we need. For me, like most, there was still lots of chipping to be done.

As Susan and I made our way to the sunroom, I explained that my back had been bothering me and asked if she would mind working on it. Susan had me lie on her massage table and started to do an energy clearing.

"No wonder it hurts, Mary. You are carrying so much stuff around. Set it down," she said, resting her hand on my shoulder reassuringly.

I sat up on the massage table, reflecting on what she was saying. I was not at all flattered by the honest, straightforward assessment. The picture-perfect life didn't look so perfect anymore. There had been so much pain associated with my divorce and my financial situation. I felt judged by those around me and depressed at the shambles my life was in.

Susan was right. I was still carrying around lots of emotional baggage, and it was manifesting in my back—emotional pain and suffering I felt I needed to hold onto in order to remind me not to keep my heart open or trust. I had a file cabinet of neatly organized memories I kept to recognize the signs and protect myself from the pain next time.

"You need to get rid of the stinkin' thinking—the program that runs in your head that tells you to make choices from fear and judgment," she said. "Remember what Jesus said: 'What you think is given unto you.'"

"You are a beautiful being, Mary. It's time to shed all that keeps you and the world from seeing the beauty that is you. Yes, you have been hurt. I am sorry that happened, but your shallow breathing is keeping you stuck in the energy you so want to get rid of. Clear the chaos out and heal. Trust that you are enough, and let go of the lack and limitations of the ego mind."

"Ugh, I have made so many mistakes. In all my trying to get it right, I have still made mistakes," I said, thinking out loud.

"We *all* make mistakes, but understand that we are not judged for them by God. We have been brainwashed to think that lack and limitation are inevitable and suffering is possibly even deserved due to our past 'sins' or errors in judgment. If we are to overcome these thoughts, we must let these blocks go. We need to release them and move into our highest potential. When we start dealing with issues that come up, instead of pushing them down and ignoring the warning signs that tell us something is wrong, we start making progress," she responded.

"We get there by connecting with our higher self, finding peace, and looking at life from a different vantage point. We can then sit in our own skin and sort through the messages in our head and start to be mindful of what we send out into the world. It all starts with the steady stream of thoughts that run through our minds," Susan explained.

Considering that all hatred driven hence,
The soul recovers radical innocence
And learns at last that it is self-delighting,
Self-appeasing, self-affrighting,
And that its own sweet will is Heaven's will.
~ William Butler Yeats

Thy Will

After Susan finished the energy clearing, we sat down in front of the sunroom window and continued our conversation. "God gave us free will to think whatever we choose, and *will* means thought. Free will is the power we have been given to determine our own thoughts, our own words, and our own actions. We don't have to make these decisions alone—remember, God is there for us, and we have a team of angels and guides who are there to assist us on our journey. But the choice is ours," Susan shared.

"On some level I have always felt that we didn't have much control over the circumstances of our lives. I thought we just worked hard and hoped and prayed for the best," I replied.

"Many people think that. But contrary to that belief, we are not separate, independent observers in the universe. We are not just passing through a moment in time in a creation that already exists. We are creator beings participating in the creation of our world. The universe is always responding to our consciousness, and what is seen and unseen both contribute," she said.

"God gave us free will to make decisions for our lives every minute of every day. *We* decide who will lead the show—the higher or ego self—and on many more levels than we understand, we determine how life unfolds. So, we need to ask ourselves, 'What do I choose?'"

I listened as Susan explained how the circumstances of our life experience come from the energy we hold in our minds and project out into the world. Every moment, the Spirit's light energy is flowing to us. We shape the energy through our thoughts and feelings and decide whether we will put a positive or negative spin on the energy based on our intentions. Each thought resonates through us. We then manifest what we are thinking about.

Like with the words Jesus shared, the Chinese proverb, "Life is an echo. What you send out comes back," describes the process. Our energy field is the bridge between the physical world and our consciousness, and our thinking feeds our experience. Our thoughts and perceptions echo through every area of our lives. But it's not just that negative thoughts create negative responses or positives create more positives—it's bigger than that. The thoughts we think become the life out in front of us that we walk into.

Much like a tuning fork, the energy we emit attracts and tunes to all other energy waves of the same frequency. We become like magnets, attracting to us what we have given to the world. We pull people, situations, and circumstances to us that reflect our thoughts and perceptions.

Our thoughts are the glue that keeps our lives in a certain state or pattern. The beliefs and expectations we choose to hold within determine which possibility manifests. The sum total of our thoughts forms the underlying belief system that creates our reality. We are shown the reflection of our consciousness in everything we see and do, and we can make anything true by activating the vibration in our energy field—cancer or violence, happiness or abundance. It all comes down to what we choose.

When we choose negativity and darkness, we are not in sync with our true nature. We upset the flow of energy within us, creating walls around our heart that fog our understanding. We manifest nonalignment that degenerates into fear, stress, and anxiety. The thicker the fog, the harder it is to see the beauty within. When we are clouded by the ego's thick, heavy fog of confusion, we may feel that we are alone and separate. Every thought, word, or action feels like trial and error. Life feels hurtful, people disappoint us, and we disappoint ourselves. We feel wounded, lonely, and unworthy, and we miss the signs that demonstrate how life works.

But if we are unhappy with the picture we are seeing, we change the thoughts we are thinking; we hold a different intention. When we understand that every thought is a choice we make and have control over, we can paint a different picture and then walk into it. We give Spirit something different to reflect, and it shows up as the landscape of our lives.

Choosing positives helps us clear the fog and opens the channel to the divine. We can then receive and process information we need to make choices in life that are to our highest good and the highest good of those around us. And when we choose to live in that joyful, abundant space, we heal our emotions, we heal our bodies, and we heal ourselves.

Truly looking at our thoughts helps us see the patterns that form beliefs and perceptions that result in actions. Changing habits and patterns helps us heal and grow and keeps us from being pulled back down into low vibrations and away from peace. The contrast between light and dark helps us see where we are supposed to be headed so the clearing can happen.

No matter what our lives looks like on the surface, we are perfect. We are beautiful works of art in progress, worthy of unconditional love, forgiveness, and freedom from judgment.

"I guess I never understood that that's what Jesus meant—that we create the circumstances of our lives with the thoughts we think," I said.

"The New Testament also states, 'Whatsoever a man soweth, he shall also reap,' which describes what we have been talking about—the universal law of cause and effect or karma," Susan responded.

I had heard about karma. It is the Sanskrit term used in Hindu and Buddhist philosophy to describe an action followed by a reaction. It is the universal law of harmony and balance that ensures every cause set in motion will at some point in the future bring about its corresponding effect.

I was aware that our actions have consequences, but I was not aware that this started at the level of thought. And like many others, I had thought karma was proof we did something wrong. But I was now learning that karma was Spirit showing us the reflection of our consciousness. As Elizabeth Clare Prophet explains in *Karma and Reincarnation: Transcending Your Past, Transforming Your Future,* "Karma is our greatest benefactor, it returns to us the good we have extended to others. It is also our greatest teacher giving us the opportunity to learn from our mistakes." Any mistake will bring about a reaction. Handle the situation positively and release any negative emotion we've attached to it, and we bring things back into balance, and the karmic loop closes.

We don't always see the effects of our thoughts and actions, because the consequences don't always show up right away—sometimes they stretch across a large span of time. But the universe keeps perfect books. So when negative circumstances show up in our lives, we know we need to shift the raw material, the thoughts and actions that created them.

"Like toddlers, we are allowed to wander freely for a while, but our karma, which stretches across lifetimes, will bring us back into alignment at some point and get us back on track. We can do it sooner and with less pain or later with larger consequences and more pain—that is our choice," Susan said.

"Remember, Mary, the toddler would continue to eat with his hands if we didn't want him to learn to use a fork. He won't learn to use the fork overnight, and there will more than likely be a mess in the kitchen, but that doesn't mean we never give him the fork again. We offer it again and again, always providing another opportunity to learn without judgment.

"It is no different on a universal level. God steps back, and, with the love of a parent, lets the child choose. With practice, the child masters the task," she continued.

I sat looking out the window at the picture-perfect autumn scene. I was beginning to understand we are responsible for every thought that goes through our minds. We own the part we play. Every single thought we have contributes to the energy that creates our current situation, our reality. Then, in fact, everything on the earth plane is a reflection of the thought behind it.

Many of us are locked into the idea that we are victims of life's circumstances. We believe things happen to us, and we had nothing to do with their creation. We call it luck or fate or explain it as "life happens." But instead, the universe is responding to our direction. As long as we point the finger at someone else, we are not taking responsibility for our choices—we are not owning what we think and feel and how we direct our energy. In the process, we are not using our God-given power to create beautiful, abundant lives.

If what Susan was telling me was true, on no level was I a victim of my circumstances. My failed relationship, declining income, and feelings of emptiness—I created them.

*Ultimately we know deeply that the other side
of every fear is freedom.
~ Marilyn Ferguson*

The Ego's Trinity Perception

Becoming more positive didn't sound difficult, but as my conversation with Susan continued, I began to see the web the ego creates and how we become entangled.

"When we let the ego run our lives, we find ourselves creating from the ego and the ego's trinity perception, which consists of strength, weakness, and fear. Creating from the ego's trinity perception, we give our true power to something outside ourselves. This perception perpetuates the stinkin' thinking we allow to run through our heads that keeps us from living in God's trinity—peace, love, and harmonious unity. We all struggle with the ego's grip in this vicious cycle. You aren't alone in this," Susan said, as a flock of crows cawed noisily outside her window.

The ego creates the illusion that we are separate from the universe, having us believe we are above or below, with more or less external power than someone else. Its internal dialogue tells us we need to have control, we need to be approved of, and we need to judge. These perceptions are perpetuated by fear—fear of not having enough or fear that someone will take from us what we feel is ours.

Driven by this perception, we strive for superficial goals outside ourselves that an ego-based world deems successful—a job, a car, a home, an attractive body, and the list goes on and on. We even find ourselves competing for God. Every day we are bombarded with messages that measure and weigh where we currently are against someone or something. Divide and conquer; separate yourself from the pack; be number one; mine, mine, mine.

Focused on competition, accumulation, and power, we find ourselves on a proverbial treadmill. We wage and gauge—how we dress, what profession we have chosen, the size of our house, the size of our bank account, if we are overweight, underweight, or have the appropriate letters behind our name. If we choose to participate, we allow the world around us to define us based on conditions. We either meet the standard and are deemed worthy of acceptance and praise or fall short and expect judgment.

Today, many things outside ourselves are revered. Many conditions are so engrained in our society that we don't see them anymore, but our emotional triggers act as huge flashing warning signs that something is wrong with the picture. When they show up, it reminds us to pay attention to whom is running the show.

Every message we perceive through the ego's trinity perception says in some way we are not good enough, don't have enough, or need to be afraid we might lose what we do have. Through the ego's lens, wealth and power are synonymous with happiness—surely life will be happier if we only have more, do more, get more. These ideas are reinforced as we put people on a pedestal who do appear to have mastered the material world and judge those as unworthy who have not. Many of us are so entrenched in this mode of thinking that we believe this is what life is truly about.

Fear drives the cycle. While acute fear is the mind-body's natural reaction to danger and fades once the danger has passed, chronic fear creates a continuum that keeps us looping through the illusion, perpetuating the motivation to act competitively with the world around us—accumulating and comparing, rather than accepting and sharing.

Lou Bougnon, author of *We Are Here to Learn,* states:

> Fear is a huge motivating factor in our world and yet it is one of the lowest vibrational frequencies and responsible for the worst atrocities. People judge for fear of being judged, rob for fear of not having enough, lie and cheat for fear of the truth, and kill for fear of being killed.

Fear is also the voice of vulnerability and doubt that leads us down a path where we feel lonely, left out, sad, depressed, and at a loss to cope.

When we face a particular challenge, our minds tend to narrow in on the issue. We focus on it and nothing else and let it keep looping through our minds again and again. All of this creates the auric fog that leaves us feeling separate from God. We feel alone in our quest to fix it or feel defeated by the issue and a victim of a chaotic world.

As a result, symptoms manifest in our bodies, alerting us to the fact that something is wrong. We might feel tightness in our chest, a lump in our throat, or a pain in our abdomen. Where the issue shows up lends clues to the source of the problem and sends us a warning signal that there is an energy constriction in that area.

It doesn't end there. People may ignore the issues that surface or blame someone else for where they are. They may lash out in their woundedness or manifest physical issues. They may bring on weight gain or weight loss, aches and pains, health issues, or even diseases, as if to say to the world, "I am wounded, please don't hurt me again." All of these issues are battle armor. Wearing this armor, we are ready and alert for the next mental, verbal, emotional, or physical attack.

Whether in the name of external power or survival, the byproducts of the ego's trinity perception include a host of low-vibrational emotions we don't want to feed, including guilt, greed, doubt, despair, judgment, and sadness. Often we feel like the damage is irreparable.

Our thinking paints the picture in front of us. The picture we choose becomes the magnet that draws similar energies, experiences, situations, and people to us. Because of this, if we are not aware that our thoughts create our world, we don't understand we might be perpetuating circumstances we would prefer to leave behind.

As I reflected on this as it related to me—the ending marriage, the striving in my business, and the continued search for an answer outside myself—I started to see the inconsistencies that existed in my life. I had been living on autopilot. I was trying to live up to a world of expectations that were not mine, showing up as someone I wasn't. Like the fly who continues to bang up against a closed and locked window even when there is a door wide open five feet away, I was walking into walls, missing open doors, and tripping on my own feet. I was stepping into every drama in front of me and had ended up with despair up to my knees.

What I hadn't realized was that I was still asking God questions from a position of "help me have more, be more, do more;" I was still looking outwardly even though everything indicated the answers came from within. I was still trying to make life happen materially without realizing that the real "secret" is that all things are possible when done through the spiritual and metaphysical principles centered in God.

"The ego's trinity perception would have us believe that life is a competition. But competition is just an illusion that creates a cycle of perceived power and overcoming weakness, of success or failure. All these things actually keep us from doing the real work we came here to do. Recognize how much power we have given the ego. Look around you—it's everywhere," Susan said.

"We don't have to look far, do we?" I replied. "It's woven into every aspect of the world we live in—political, financial, corporate, rites of passage, and even religion."

"You're right," she responded. "It seems anything can be used. Every day we're bombarded with the messages that cloud our thinking and reinforce the problem. We may feel deep within that something is lacking in our lives. Yet, we may not realize what is really missing, because collective agreement tells us this is how life works—this is what life is about. It would have us believe we'll be happy if we accumulate more and more. And while money may be able to buy us all sorts of things, it cannot buy us a higher vibration, and *that* is our goal as souls.

"Understand that nothing that is based in fear is of the mind of God, and contaminated thoughts limit our inner power, joy, and health. It's a struggle not to be affected in a consumer-based society. We are continually told we aren't enough and spiral until we decide to make a change," Susan said.

"I can see the contradiction and how easy it is to get entangled in these beliefs and forget that above the chaos, there is a God who loves us unconditionally," I replied. We are all equal in the eyes of God. With him, we know we are never alone. In him, we know we are unconditionally loved. Through his eyes, we know we are absolutely perfect wherever we find ourselves on our journey.

"We are entering a new consciousness now. We are moving beyond the five senses to a multisensory experience, and we need to start creating differently. It starts by clearing out the darkness in the corners of our own minds and raising our own vibration. It happens when we look beyond the bondage that anchors us to the ego," Susan explained.

I was fascinated, and when I took the concepts and expanded them across humanity, I wondered, "So everything is energy, and the source of the love, peace, and light energy we seek is our God. Then, if we can learn to express those divine qualities in our lives, heaven on Earth must be possible, right?"

"Remember that is why Jesus was sent," she said. "Jesus came to this plane to demonstrate for us that true enlightenment and living in a state of divine grace is possible here on Earth. His life is meant to be our example for how to live and express the divine within us, our true power, through life experiences. Yes, heaven on Earth is possible if we all work toward peace. It is what we are supposed to be creating.

"Remember, when we think as he would have us think and live as he would have us live, thy will *will* be done in Earth as it is in heaven," Susan said.

"Thy will be done in Earth as it is in heaven..." I trailed off, thinking about what the line from the Lord's Prayer meant, as if I was hearing it for the first time. How many times had I said those words and never thought through their actual meaning—never realized how much information they held about how life really works?

"I actually see the Father as love, the son as peace, and the Holy Spirit as harmonious unity," she said. "We are to take our place in that trinity, as peaceful, humane beings."

"Then God's will is for us to create peace on Earth. Jesus, the Prince of Peace, came to show us how—of course! The wooden statue shows Jesus cradling God's children. The message: we need to hew away to reveal our true essence and express it out in the world—the peace we carry with us that is often hidden under the ego's veil. *Thy will* is to create peace on Earth. And when we overcome our fears, we find freedom. This is so enlightening!" I said.

Susan smiled. "Greater understanding is really what enlightenment means. The more enlightened the soul, the higher it vibrates. Our sensory perception then becomes more in tune with what lies beyond the physical world, and we are aware of a greater orchestration of life and love. This is really about the ultimate power—the power we have given away, because we have not learned to conquer fear. And when we allow people and society to define who we are, we miss the opportunity to know the person we are meant to be."

I tried to summarize, "So we are here to grow as souls and move into our oneness with God. This is accomplished through the life lessons our guides put out in front of us. The lessons help us see where the ego-based perception grips our lives and constricts our hearts."

"How we handle those lessons is determined by our thoughts and perceptions. In order to advance as souls, we sort through those thoughts and, where needed, think differently. We make choices that are more in line with God's will and not based in fear and the ego's trinity perception," Susan said.

"And when we create peace within, it is reflected in our lives and out in the world," I responded.

The keys to turning life's circumstances around were right under my nose. Jesus had told us. Yet like so many of us, I was unaware of the depth of the message.

Then what do I really choose? I thought. *If I peel back all the voices from the world outside me—all the shoulds and musts imposed out there—what does my higher self and God truly choose for this life? Peace may be the goal, but how do I get there?*

On a day like this, surely I have the faith of a mustard seed. The strength to break through a seemingly impenetrable surface and emerge victoriously into the light on the other side. Today, I'll abandon my armor and fears and see only the truth in every experience. The beauty and harmony that forms the foundation of all.
~ Melissa

Chipping at the Ego

Unearthing my true essence became my main focus. Like Michelangelo who chipped away at a block of marble, removing bit by bit everything that hid the masterpiece within, I chipped away at my ego's perception to find my true self, chiseling away at all the pain I now understood I created.

It became my silent vow to take a different approach to life moving forward. Instead of being the mighty oak standing solid, strong, and unbending, I would lean into life, flexing with it and letting life flow. I would become the sapling that finds resilience by bending with the breeze. I would welcome it with open arms, surrendering to the process and working to let go of anything that disturbed my peace.

Identifying and unraveling the ego self was a big decision and yet no decision at all. It is inevitable really. It is an ongoing process that involves a level of trust and a willingness to be open to the experience—not trying to make things happen but allowing them to happen. I prayed:

Dear Spirit,

Awaken my heart. Transform my emotions and illuminate my mind so that I may think as you would have me think, and act as you would have me act, and be who you would have me be today. Amen

I became more open and aware of life as it unfolded, all the while identifying with the phoenix that crashed and burned and rose again. I was that phoenix. I saw signs of it everywhere and knew it with all my heart. I was open to the lessons in front of me, knowing that, like the phoenix, I too would soar again.

When I arrived home after meeting with Susan that day, I was tired and weary and laid down for a nap. In my mind's eye, I saw a beautiful, white butterfly floating toward me. I stood very still so it would land near me. As the butterfly grew closer, it transformed into an eagle. It was unlike any eagle I'd ever seen—his head and entire body were pure white and covered in soft, silky feathers. The eagle landed on my shoulder and let me stroke his beak. He let me hold him and cradle him like a baby. We shared a moment of warmth, mutual love, and respect.

When I later told Susan about my experience, she explained the eagle was White Eagle, the spirit guide who is known as the "Task Master." White Eagle had come to guide me through the process of releasing my fears and inhibitions. Looking back I realized he had been with me for some time already. He had arrived the day the eagle landed on the side of the road as I drove home from the airport after my 9/11 trip to Paris. I was just finally open enough to realize he was there.

White Eagle became a fixture in my life, sharing wisdom and providing guidance. The lessons put in front of me were tough. My ego was often bruised. But White Eagle's presence reminded me that our lessons are not meant to hurt us but rather to reveal our authentic selves.

Over time, White Eagle showed me that everything I truly needed I already held within me. My vibration was raised over and over again until my body felt light. Layer after layer was pulled back. Every time, I was, and continue to be, amazed at the immensity and grace of the truth seen in greater and greater clarity.

What sculpture is to a block of marble,
education is to a human soul.
~ Joseph Addison

Spiritual Sculpting Tools

Fall days grew shorter, and the bright colors of autumn faded. Leafless and budless trees patterned the countryside. Their solid trunks and branches no longer hidden, they stood tall and proud. While the earth was preparing to sleep, I felt like I was finally waking up.

In and out, weeks and months, I was guided. Lesson after lesson helped me understand that every situation is a lesson in how to respond to life more perfectly. Framed in this understanding, I began to move through the situations that presented themselves, asking, "What is this situation really about?" and "What am I supposed to learn from this?" Through these questions, a set of spiritual sculpting tools emerged. These tools helped me nurture what I wanted to thrive and identify and chip away at what no longer served me. The spiritual tools I use to hew away at the ego's trinity perception to reveal my true essence follow.

Recognize Gentle Nudges and Cosmic Two-by-Fours
Thoughts are the building blocks of our lives. Linked together, they are the stream of consciousness that creates our experience. To change that experience, we pull apart the stream, analyze our thoughts, and consciously choose what we want to keep and what we want to discard.

When we take control of our thoughts, we take control of the reality we are creating. When we quiet our minds, we quiet any interference. When negative impulses are not met with conscious thoughts, they do not have the negative impact on our lives they would otherwise. When our intentions are pure and our actions hold the Christ consciousness above our own earthly desires, we aren't running into walls and retracing our steps. There are fewer karmic games of chutes and ladders with the higher self leading the way; there is no karmic reaction being created to trigger an effect to live later on.

Every negatively charged thought we experience tells us something about ourselves that keeps us from a higher vibration. Really looking at them helps us identify beliefs and perceptions and release blocks within ourselves, so we can change, and our light can grow.

It starts with recognizing the signs that we are no longer at peace. We often refer to those signs as suffering. And in the end, like with thoughts, the suffering we attach to them is a choice. Byron Katie says in *Loving What Is,* "All suffering is optional..." She explains:

> Anytime we experience a stressful feeling—anything from mild discomfort to intense sorrow, rage, or despair—we can be certain that there is a specific thought causing our reaction, whether or not we are conscious of it. The way we end the stress is to investigate the thinking that lies behind it.

Sometimes the signs are gentle nudges that tell us a thought or belief needs to change. Others are like cosmic two-by-fours that knock us upside the head and demand a greater call to action. Still recognizing that a thought is causing the issue is one thing—being still and figuring out what is prompting it is another. At times it can take discernment to see past the surface problem and get to the root cause; some roots run very deep, but the signs will show up in the landscape of our lives, so they can be identified and excavated.

Make Conscious Choices

Thoughts themselves hold no positive or negative vibrational charge. Our happiness or our suffering is determined by the emotion we attach to our thoughts based on our perception. Since positives are what we seek, the negatives that come to the surface are what we examine and remove. Monitoring our energy moment by moment, we create greater emotional awareness and learn to make conscious choices on how we direct our energy.

When something in life triggers fear, sadness, or any negative emotion, internally say, "Stop!" View the world through the lens of the experience, and filter what is happening. Single out the thought that is causing the issue, the suffering. Take a moment to really feel the thought and the associated emotion. Then decide if you want to consciously change it. Ask yourself, "Is this what I truly choose?" If it is a negative thought, ask yourself, "Do I choose to give up my personal power to this fearful or unloving thought?"

Then, like the weed that it is, remove the thought and replace it with a more positive, more loving thought. Picture the energy shifting in your body. See yellow, smiley faces on every cell to instill happiness, or visualize the blue light of peace filling you and moving you into a more blissful state.

My daughters were growing up, and their life experiences provided opportunities to apply the concepts I, myself, was learning. One night I came home to find my older daughter, who had just finished the sixth grade, lying on her bed staring at the wall. I walked in and sat next to her and asked her what was wrong. She recounted the events of a birthday party she had been to that afternoon. The party was for a new friend she had recently made who was connected to a different group of friends. She shared that she didn't feel the same level of confidence with this new group of people she normally did.

I talked to her about the thoughts that were going through her head and asked her how she would feel if she could stop thinking the thought that she didn't have confidence. She looked at me and said with a smile, "I think I should squash the thought like a bug." We laughed at the image of the downtrodden thought being squashed, and a smile returned to her face. The idea that she didn't have confidence was gone, and my bubbly daughter returned. Mission accomplished.

When we let go of old programming, we allow change to take place; when we remove that which might otherwise choke off the joy, the laughter, and the love we want to flourish, we can then move forward with an open heart in absolute faith that we will be OK.

Say and affirm, "I am choosing differently now," understanding that wanting something different is not about what's right or wrong. Those things only exist in our own perception. But when we stop the cycle, we once again remember who we really are. When we remember who we are, we find peace again. And when we find what vibrates as truth for us, we can discard everything else. It is the quality and value of our lives that we seek, defined from within us and portrayed as a tapestry of light around us. Our soul's expression is not defined by fear; it's defined by the eternal light of love.

It's important to remember that all thoughts and emotions that result in stress and anxiety bring us more of the same. They continue to spiral downward, causing more and more issues in our lives—both emotional and physical—until we break the cycle. We can shift the energy moving through us when we are aware of our emotions. When we clear out negative emotional energy we have hung onto, we aren't so overwhelmed anymore. The real work happens when we look at what the situation brought up within us—how we feel and the reaction it triggers.

Moving forward, we choose thoughts, words, and actions that add to life, like hope, faith, joy, and generosity, and let go of those that vibrate doubt, skepticism, bitterness, greed, sadness, and despair. We ask the divine to cancel out and dissolve the energy of past intentions we do not want to be part of our present or future reality.

The following questions helped me sort through the details of my life. Where suffering appears in your life, you can use these questions as guidelines to help discern the lessons and the meaning behind them.

1. Am I Living in the Present?
If we find that in the moment we would rather be somewhere else, we are being pulled from our inner peace and are not living in the present. When this happens, parts of us contract or shut down, and energy is unable to flow through us unconstrained.

We can remember the past, but we cannot change it. We can anticipate the future, but it doesn't serve us to live a life that has not yet arrived. What is true is what *is* happening now and not what we think *should* be happening. When we are no longer wishing our present away or missing it by reliving a past or a future we have no control over anyway, we find harmony with ourselves.

In order to create a space where peace, love, and abundance can thrive, we find blessings in the now. We start fresh each moment, wholeheartedly and unconflicted. Seeing the beauty of the now, we anchor it in and state the intention, "It's a brand-new moment, and I'm going to embrace being me."

I was born into a family with loving parents and three older brothers. I remember my mom telling me that they were happy with their family but that my dad really wanted daughters, so they tried for more children. I was born five years after my closest brother, and my sister was born five years after me.

But even before I was born, circumstances in my parents' lives set in motion what my childhood would be like. My dad had had his first heart attack at thirty-four, and my mom, realizing that she might have to raise kids on her own, went back to school and back to work. That meant that there was often no parent around when I was growing up. When my mom was home, she never seemed to be very happy.

Looking back, I was sure the thought of raising five kids by herself contributed to my mother's stress level. But as a child, I didn't have that perspective. I was often alone and felt disconnected. I vividly remembered the feelings and wanted something very different for my children—to be around when and if they needed me and limit the amount of separateness they might feel. Yes, I wanted different, but this was not it. I was now a single mother raising two children, and it was challenging. Money was tight as I tried to be there for them in ways my parents had not been able to, as well as in ways they were. So often I pined for a different and easier life.

I tried to give my kids what I could materially and experientially, and I told them often that their mommy loved them "always and forever no matter what." I wanted them to have a different life, yet I was focused on past circumstances that got me where I was instead of showing up in the moment and creating differently. I instead needed to learn to be present—it's really the only place from which true progress happens. All creation is born in the now, and every moment we are given the opportunity to choose differently.

2. Am I Accepting What I Don't Have Control Over?
"One of the greatest sources of unhappiness people have is accepting things as they are," Susan said. "Often when we see something we don't like, we wish it could be different, and we cry out for something better."

If we listen to ourselves and those around us, we'll often hear conditions like, "She should have called," "He shouldn't be so mean," and "She shouldn't treat people like that." But the truth is, those things are often out of our control and struggling against or lamenting over them doesn't get us anywhere. We create our own reality, but everyone else has free will in the same way we do. We do not have control over what someone else decides to do or not do any more than we have control over the order of the seasons—winter will always follow fall. Nature and natural law demonstrate this for us all the time. Gravity anchors our physical body to the ground, and the cycle of life continues whether we agree with it or not.

Surrendering to life means allowing it to unfold. But surrendering is not about cowering in the physical sense of the word, nor is it about giving up. It's more about accepting, allowing, and detaching from our expectations and a need to change things. Surrendering is about letting go of outcomes—it's about understanding that what we perceive to be imperfect is really perfect just as it is. Everything has a synchronicity and is the way it is for a reason beyond our understanding. If we release our need to control things, we find that each moment and every situation holds a blessing whether it be patience, nonjudgment, joy, or the opportunity for perfect peace.

My older daughter had her first love relationship. It was fun to watch her beam with joy as she got to know this young man. She, herself, had called it puppy love.

They spent lots of time together going to movies, spending time with friends, and just hanging out together, playing games. Unfortunately, they started to have issues. Friends were jealous, and his parents didn't feel as if he was ready to be in a relationship. As arguments ensued, my daughter told the boyfriend that she thought it would be a good idea to break up. They agreed, and it ended. But once it was over, my daughter regretted her decision and reached out to him with hopes that they could reconcile. Unfortunately, he said no.

I watched her struggle to accept the situation as she replayed the events over and over in her mind, spiraling into a deep sadness. Through her tears and pain, she shared with me that she wished she had done things differently. She explained that she didn't understand why they couldn't be together. Still, there were lots of influences beyond her control.

I held her close and explained that it was OK—there would be others. She said she wished she hadn't broken up with him. I explained that, unfortunately, we can't go back. At times we all wish we could go back, but we have to accept where we are and move forward.

I wished I could stop the pain she was feeling, but I knew she was learning a lot from the situation, and in time she would heal.

3. Am I Living My Own Life?

"We are often so busy worrying about where everyone else is in their lives that we aren't figuring our own stuff out," Susan said in one of our sessions. "When we spend our time focused on what other people are doing, or if they are showing up for us the way we think they should, we aren't really even living. We are focused on their lives. Meanwhile no one is living ours. In the process, we have limited our own ability to create and have given our power away.

"When we are worried about how someone else is living his or her life, we feel separate. We are not maintaining our connection with Spirit. If you find yourself guilty of this, reconnect and breathe in peace. Clear out the clutter, and move back into the now. It will help you get back on track," Susan explained.

I understood what she was saying. I was now focused on healing my life and figuring out who I was. In the process, I had, for all intents and purposes, set my business aside. So while my colleagues were working, and their incomes were growing, my income was still dropping, and it felt like the floor was falling out underneath me.

It may be an ego benchmark, but watching my colleagues was tough at times. I was pulled to get back to work. Still, I knew I couldn't worry about it—unless I healed my life, none of it would matter anyway. And I wasn't sure if this was where I was supposed to be anymore...*Dear God, what is my purpose on Earth? Where do I go from here?*

As if she knew what I was thinking, Susan added, "We also need to look at why we're acting the way we are. Why are we doing the things we are doing? Are we acting because someone else thinks something is right for us or because our higher self thinks it is? At times we are so wrapped up in other people's perceptions, we forget to ask ourselves, 'Does this vibrate as truth for me?' 'Is this truly what I choose?'

"Remember to ask yourself, 'What do *I* choose?' Stay anchored in the understanding that God is guiding our lives. If we don't need to be fed by other people or pulled by something outside ourselves, we can make progress on our path.

"When you feel pulled in a direction you aren't meant to go, remember to tell yourself, 'It doesn't matter what you think, I know.' The 'I know' I am referring to is not the arrogance of the ego, but the deep understanding of Spirit. The understanding that (when we open to it) provides the stepping-stones to show us our truths," she said.

4. What Does the Mirror's Reflection Show Me?

Everything in life is a reflection of what we have given to it. Spiritual mirrors reflect in the outer world who we truly are on the inner plane—our unique experiences, beliefs, and perceptions. The mirror's reflection is the filter we use to sort through our emotions and responses. We use spiritual mirrors to translate what we understand about every person we meet, every situation we face—all of life.

The emotions we feel when we are interacting with others are ours. We bring them to the surface based on thoughts, beliefs, and perceptions we hold. They really have nothing to do with anyone else. And what other people think about us in any given situation is really about them, unless we make their beliefs, perceptions and energy ours.

When situations surface that spark conflict or suffering, we use mirrors to look at how the situation reflects back on us. Then we look at the world and see how it reflects on others and the collective consciousness around us.

If we look at our beliefs—really look at them as emotion brings them to the surface—we can ask ourselves: Is this true or is this merely an illusion? Is this what my heart truly chooses, or is this perception born in the ego's trinity perception? Then we can figure out why we created that perception. We can sort through where the perception reflects back on our life and if it is to our highest good to hang on to it.

Then moving forward, we will become more aware when negative thoughts and emotions take root and define our experience. We will notice how negatives create more negatives and how the fear we see around us reflects the fear we create in our own minds. The same is true of positives. Anchoring positive thoughts and experiences into our lives allows us to move into a more positive experience moving forward.

"Mirrors can be hard, but they are important to our progress as souls," Susan explained in a discussion we had one day. "As we interact with others, it's easy to get caught up in the idea that it's other people who have issues and to think that their problems are causing our suffering. If *they* would just change, life would be so much better. So often we don't look at the issues that come up in situations with others, we just change the people. We think if we bring in new people, life will be different, but then we have missed the lesson. It's not really about other people but the thoughts and perceptions that are in *our* program that we tend to attach to others.

"Typically, we can find lots of people who will tell us that it's really the other person who has issues and is the problem. The truth is people who tend to push our buttons the most are generally our greatest teachers. They are mirrors reflecting back to us what needs to be revealed about ourselves; we project our ideas and beliefs about how we think the world should look onto other people," she continued. "Identifying what we don't like in others helps us look deeper inside ourselves for similar traits and challenges that need healing, balancing, or changing.

"When we find a perception that is based in an illusion, we can look for opportunities to trace the energy line back to its source. We can then see where the perception originated and pull the belief out, root and all. When the weeds are truly removed, they no longer choke off that which we truly choose. Once we see where they came from and our attachment to them, we can move into the next moment, choosing differently. When we have truly let go, if the perception resurfaces, the emotional attachment is no longer there," Susan said.

"Look in the mirror, Mary. It will show you what is real and what is just a story your ego is telling you about what something in your past or future means—ego-based thoughts that can hold us back from our true potential," she said.

I understood. I had pretty much done just that.

In the final days of my divorce, I had met someone new—a doctor who represented everything I thought I wanted in life in terms of success and lifestyle and another chance at happiness. My heart had been breaking on the inside, but I held it together on the outside, so I could have a chance to get to know this person who had what I had thought life was all about—the big house, the string of exotic cars, the landscape of experiences that the world often labels as "success" and yet was someone who made time to study the Bible daily.

As the doctor and I had gotten to know each other, we spent time exploring new restaurants, going for long walks, and driving in the flavor-of-the-day exotic car through the countryside. We had a great time, and it was tempting to think that this might be the answer. It wasn't until we took a trip to Tuscany together that the message came through loud and clear that that was not the case. The situation not only was a great example of mirrors but also demonstrated that my guides were busy sending me signs that my life may be headed in a direction I shouldn't be going.

On our trip to Italy, we spent time in a villa in Florence, toured Tuscany, and finished our trip exploring Portofino with a group of the doctor's friends. We were all smiles and holding hands as we made our way to Florence, but that didn't last. Things started to happen.

The first sign was that my luggage didn't show up when we arrived in Florence. So, instead of joining the group to see Michelangelo's *David*, I spent the afternoon buying socks and underwear. Shopping in Italy? Sure! This kind of shopping? No thanks.

The second sign was not as subtle. As we returned to the room one night after dinner, a suitcase was sitting in the entryway. It seemed as if my luggage had finally arrived. Yet, with closer examination we realized the suitcase, with *my* luggage tag attached, wasn't mine. Apparently, the airline had delivered someone else's luggage, and mine had gone to California! (I had enough baggage of my own at this point—I didn't need to take on someone else's.)

The subtle and not-so-subtle messages continued. Staff at every hotel we stayed at asked if they could help me, as if I was not a guest there. Each apologized profusely when they realized that I was, in fact, staying in their hotel. To top things off, someone stole a bracelet the doctor had given me from the hotel room, *and* I was getting sick. With everything that had already happened on the trip, I really didn't want the doctor or anyone else on the tour to know I was growing more and more ill. Like an *I Love Lucy* episode, I started to look ridiculous as I tried to hide what was really going on.

It was the last stop on our trip, Portofino, and the doctor and I decided to stay in the village while the rest of the group went on a boat tour of the Italian Riviera. We sat together on the hotel balcony overlooking the Mediterranean, enjoying coffee and reading. The doctor asked me to listen as he quoted the Bible. He then explained how he felt women were supposed to be submissive.

I was in shock. I had been trying to find my own voice and was now being told that because of my gender, I wasn't supposed to have one! If we are truly all equal in the eyes of God, then how could this be true?

Message finally delivered. This was not where I was supposed to be. It wasn't that I didn't belong in these places but that I hadn't shown up as my authentic self or with the right companion. My journey was not about shifting to a new partner or different income bracket but letting go of my ego baggage, not taking on anyone else's, and showing up as my true self. As the trip came to an end, so did the relationship.

Thinking about this experience, I could see that I had done exactly what Susan was talking about—I had gone out and found another relationship that very much reflected the one I had ended. Thinking about my ex-husband, Carl, I realized there was still more to learn from our relationship. I didn't know it would mean we would end up a couple again, but I did want to understand how my thinking had contributed to our issues. I did want to find peace in that relationship.

My daughter came to me one afternoon to tell me that her sister had told her she was fat. I understood the ego's weights and measures...not smart, not pretty, not popular...the comments were as varied as the day is long.

"Sweetheart, you know better than anyone who you are. Is she right?"

Finally stopping the ego comparison that no one ever really wins, she answered, "No Mommy, she's not."

"Of course she's not," I responded, hugging her.

Most often my daughters can see that these are just stories that reflect perceptions that aren't real. They are illusions that have no bearing on reality and clearly have nothing to do with who they really are. I prayed they would remember this as they grew.

If I could teach them this, perhaps they would never let the fear of being judged let them sink as low as I had during my divorce, putting on a tough exterior, trying to hide that my life had become an empty shell. Only a few friends and family members knew the depth of my depression and called me to make sure I realized I still mattered. Susan, those friends, and the spiritual network that guided me had helped me see glimpses of the real me and my truth worth. Through that lens, I was finding clarity and inner peace and the sparks of hope and happiness I didn't know were there. Unraveling judgment would take some work for me, but having a better understanding of who I was at my core, I was finding I was up for the challenge.

I went out for dinner with a girlfriend I hadn't seen in a while. We sat and caught up. She shared that she had health issues she was seeing a doctor for. She updated me on her husband's heart issues and then explained that one of her sons had also recently been diagnosed with cancer. There seemed to be so much illness and sadness in her family. I felt compassion for her, but it seemed clear that she felt like a victim of life. I wondered where that all stemmed from and how much of it was in her conscious control.

Then it was my turn. I shared updates on my kids and work and life. But as I listened to myself, really listened to what I was saying, I realized how negative I sounded. I hadn't realized before that I was doing this. Was this the underlying source of my problems and a reflection of a deeper belief system within me I needed to shake? Obviously, it didn't vibrate very highly. It didn't make me feel very peaceful either. Did my friend and I share the same vibrational frequency, and was that the reason why we related to each other? Would we still be friends if I changed my tune? Regardless, I realized now what I was doing and that it needed to change so I could change. I chose to be positive, loving, and kind. I get to choose!

It had been a couple of years since our divorce, and the tension between my ex and I had eased. I decided to take a closer look at why our marriage fell apart. In my heart I knew I needed to heal any hurts that still remained. And maybe, just maybe, there was still something there. So I faced my fears and decided to figure out what was left to learn from this relationship.

Carl and I had decided during the divorce that our daughters would remain our first priority. We would do our best to get past our issues and show up as best we could for them. As a result, we found ourselves supporting each other in other areas of our lives as well. Though we had never stopped going to school conferences together, and we often sat next to each other at the girls' plays, concerts, and sporting events, we were obviously separate. But now I invited Carl to hang out more with the girls and me—having game nights, taking our daughters golfing, and having dinner as a family.

As we started to spend more time together, people around us looked at us and wondered what the heck we were doing. Many people told us just how crazy they thought we were. We were often asked, "Why, if you are divorced, would you choose to have any sort of relationship with your ex?"

I looked past it. I was not sure about him, but I wanted to really understand what was in my heart and see what feelings were still there. I also knew I didn't want to attract the same lessons again. I wanted to truly see what these lessons showed me about myself and move past them. I wanted to forgive Carl and myself and release all the pain associated with the failed marriage. I wanted to move into my own creative power and highest truth. I hoped Carl would also let go of his pain and move into something different as well, whether it was with me or someone else. Still, I knew his spiritual growth was out of my control.

The girls and I had often traveled to the Twin Cities to visit my mom. Over time I noticed subtle differences in her, but it was now becoming clear that my mom's memory wasn't what it used to be.

My brothers and sister held a phone conference to discuss the situation, and we each shared our views. While we all wanted to honor our mother and ensure that if her memory failed her, she was safe. We all had different opinions about what was really going on.

One by one, we shared our views. When it was my turn, I offered mine. But as we closed the conversation, I felt as if my ideas had been dismissed. After I hung up the phone, I replayed our discussion in my head. I didn't feel like I was being heard, and that was an important part of feeling valued and successful for me. I didn't feel like I had a voice. The pain in my throat confirmed that I was feeling as if my siblings hadn't listened to me.

I was sad and couldn't hide my pain from my kids. Seeing my distress, my younger daughter, who was now eight, got up from the game she was playing with her sister on the floor. She crossed the room and curled up next to me. "Mom, it doesn't matter what other people think. It matters what you know in your heart." Then off she went to join her sister again on the floor.

Wow! My old-soul daughters always seemed to know exactly what was going on. That one comment shifted me as I realized I still needed to be fed—acknowledged and understood outside myself. In the end, it was OK my siblings didn't realize where I was in all of this, and it was only a problem, because I had decided it was one. I looked past their perceptions (or how I perceived them to be), remembering we are all a work in progress.

When I allowed the perception to fade, in many ways, so did the issue. And as it did, I felt more confident in myself. In turn, I was more aware of my mother in her situation. I could see in a much greater way that it was more important now to understand the place she found herself in and to be a source of compassion for her.

The Christmas season was around the corner, and the local department stores were looking for extra help for the shopping season, and I decided to take a seasonal position, working at a perfume counter at one of the stores. In talking with coworkers, a few of us discovered we were all spending Thanksgiving alone and decided to spend the holiday together instead. I offered my home as a place for us to gather.

Thanksgiving eve was filled with shopping and baking and cleaning. As I was getting my younger daughter ready for bed, I discovered that she hadn't brushed her teeth, so we went into the bathroom together to brush and floss.

We stood next to each other looking in the mirror and watching each other, smiling and giggling. But as I flossed my lower teeth, the floss got caught under a lower front crown, and the crown popped off. I heard it ping as it bounced off something and disappeared.

I looked in the mirror at the gaping hole in my smile and panicked. It was a holiday weekend. I had a houseful of people coming to dinner the next day, and I had to work Black Friday at the department store!

Together my daughter and I combed the bathroom looking for the crown, but it was nowhere to be found. I called my dentist's emergency number. No answer. I waited and called again. No returned call. I waited and waited for the dentist to call. Nothing.

I tried stuffing the empty space with cotton. That worked fine until I opened my mouth to talk or eat or drink. With as much grace as I could muster, I entertained Thanksgiving Day and found the courage to work the perfume counter on Friday—I made it through.

As I walked out to the parking lot after my Black Friday shift, I felt the nudge to look at the sky. When I did, I saw the image of the phoenix in the clouds above, and the message I received was two-fold: First, you are a beautiful being regardless. Don't let something small and insignificant keep you from feeling that. Second, you *are* the phoenix, preparing to fly.

I knew that once again my prayers had been heard. I had asked God to show me to myself, and that was what was happening. This lesson was a mirror to show me my own judgment. I prayed that my lessons be a little smaller for a while. I wanted to grow as a soul, but I felt like I had bitten off more than I could chew.

I knew I was often critical of my physical appearance; it was a judgment I held. I thought back to where that judgment originated. There was a lot there to sort through, but in a not-so-subtle way, this experience mirrored that judgment loud and clear. How often had I not done something in my life for fear of being judged for it? How often had I passed judgment on others?

I felt like I had been hit with another cosmic two-by-four and called Susan to get advice.

"It's so important for us to know ourselves clearly. When we do, we don't get locked into someone else's opinion of us. We accept ourselves wherever we find ourselves. We acknowledge others wherever they are on their path with unconditional love and no judgment. We give ourselves and others the chance to just 'be,'" Susan said.

"When we are no longer scared to just 'be,' it no longer matters what others think of us or what they say about us. When others judge us, we realize that their thoughts and judgments are more a reflection of their own need to grow than ours. The more in-tune we become, the more we let go of others' ideas and perceptions and how they show up in life.

"Your guides want you to know that this situation didn't happen to you to hurt you but merely to show you to yourself. Remember that moments of struggle hold moments of triumph and victory. Don't look at it as a punishment. It is only a demonstration that helped you understand an aspect of yourself. Sometimes the very compression we are experiencing is so uncomfortable that it helps move us to something else.

"Understand that if we perceive an issue as difficult and uncomfortable, we have judged the experience as well. In judging it we have made it what it is. Thoughts and perceptions are harmless unless we believe and judge them and feed them energy. When we judge them, we lock them into reality. We give them power!" she said.

"Learn to look at situations, and instead of judging them, say to yourself, 'Isn't that interesting.' When you are OK with where you are, you are free to move on to something else. When there is no judgment, things can change. And when you heal that judgment in an area of your life, that judgment and pattern will be healed in every area of your life it touches.

"And don't judge or criticize yourself or your thoughts. Instead be congruent with your thoughts, working with them and not against them. Then centered in God's image, with him as the mirror of your worth, fear and judgment will fall away. Reach deep down and bring up your connection and ask, 'Is this really the way I see it, or is this a lack of trust?' In the end, you will find that all issues fall away when you are connected, and it's only your perception run by ego that creates a problem. It's your perception that makes the situation difficult and uncomfortable. You think and perceive it to be so, and it becomes real.

"Move back into the present. Find joy and acceptance in the now. Remember to look at every person or situation and know that everyone is exactly where they are for a reason. Simply say, 'That's interesting.' Your need to judge will disappear. Your need to control will vanish. Every issue in our lives becomes a blessing, and the awareness we gain by understanding the internal cause and effect helps us move from a place of suffering to a place of peace," she explained.

Over time I learned to recognize and isolate my thoughts. I could cancel a message and replace it with a more positive thought. I identified and released conditional thoughts based in the ego's trinity perception, formed when we say, "I...because." I let go of perceptions like "She doesn't like me," "What was he thinking?" and "Why didn't she call?" I continued to detangle from past energies and ask myself, "What do I choose now?" I worked through emotions and released those that were unwanted. I anchored back in peace, love, and light. My new mantra became "I am the master of my own thoughts, words, and emotions."

Reflecting on my spiritual journey, I realized that the entire experience was also a mirror. It felt as if I was being sent on a vision quest. Vision quests are common in Native American culture. When an individual reaches a certain maturity, they are sent out into the wilderness for a period of time in order to tune into the Spirit world, to commune with nature, and to find what the Creator intends for their life. The quest often involves fasting and is a test of stamina that prepares them for the rest of their journey.

I did feel as if I was living in a form of wilderness, even if it was in the middle of town. As with traditional American Indian vision quests, I felt as if I was being tested as the old life was stripped away, the old consciousness excavated, so that new understanding could be revealed. My quest also involved finding my way with limited resources and, at times, I felt pushed to my limits. But remembering the work would eventually need to be done, I drew on the image of the eagle lying in my arms. I pressed through, focused on learning what was in front of me, and from a place deep within, I heard a voice tell me I needn't be scared. I would be provided with what I needed.

In vision quests, faith is cultivated as we walk a wire between the perceptions of the higher and ego self. But for me, there was no direction but forward. In my heart, I heard an echo, "*I can do all things through Christ who strengthens me.*" Keep moving forward...

Working with mirrors is an ongoing process. We catch ourselves when we recognize we are going down a negative path. We replace the negatives with more positive, loving thoughts and release the attached suffering. The more we chip away, the more we find that even the weeds are beautiful in their own way. No, we don't want to keep them, or they would choke off what we want to flourish, but obstacles and challenges teach us patience, gratitude, and grace. They can be the impetus we need to create a life of wholeness and abundance. Every bit of pressure in our lives brings us an opportunity to burst forth and show our true selves to the world, expanding outward instead of contracting inward.

5. Is This Mine?

As the light within us grows, our energy field expands further beyond ourselves. The larger and clearer our field, the more heightened our intuition. We become more and more sensitive to the subtle energies around us. The more sensitive we are, the more important it is to be able to differentiate what belongs to us and what belongs to someone else, so we don't take on issues that aren't ours or become contaminated by lower energies.

While I wasn't as involved in my business now, I still maintained some involvement. One night when I was attending a business presentation, I was sitting and quietly taking notes. Suddenly out of nowhere I heard, "Oh my God, it's sales!" go through my mind. *"Of course it's sales!"* I thought to myself, *"I **know** it's sales! Why would I think that?"* Then it occurred to me that that thought didn't even belong to me. I had just tapped into someone else's thoughts.

Another example of this happened when I was attending a seminar in Chicago. From the moment I entered the conference room, I felt an overwhelming amount of anxiety. No matter how much deep breathing I did, I couldn't shake it. It got to the point where I started professing my anxiety to those around me, not realizing consciously that I was trying to release it.

Realizing I was having a hard time shaking the feeling, I walked outside and called Susan. She explained that what I was feeling wasn't even mine. I was tapping into the energy of those around me. "You subconsciously asked what was going on in the room and tapped into that energy. Remember to pull up your peace first and then look at what is going on around you. Observe the energy and then let go of it. Do not hang on to it and claim it as your own.

"The higher our vibration and the cleaner our energy, the more we sense. The bigger our light, the more we can tap into other people's thoughts, feelings, story lines, and even physical symptoms," she said. "Make sure you are protected. You want to know which messages are yours and which are someone else's. And then work on what *you* truly created.

"When you realize that you are feeling something that doesn't belong to you, learn to recognize it. And if you choose to look at what is going on with someone else, observe it and then release it. You do not have to hang on to it as if it's yours. Feel compassion and understanding, but don't take it on. And if you want others to see what they are creating themselves, put up mirrors. In this way, the energy reflects back on them, and they see what they are projecting."

6. Survey Your Progress

Our spiritual journey is an ongoing process. As we peel back the layers of realization, more thoughts and emotions surface. Chipping and chiseling, we apply what we have learned and regain more and more of our own truths. By continually adjusting our perception of reality to what we currently understand, we can continue to grow, evolve, and become. It's important to keep only what resonates with where we are right now and discard the rest.

As I released blocks in my heart, the change rippled through my entire life, and little by little, every corner was touched positively. As a result, I cleaned up my office, my closet, and my diet. I found peace in relationships with friends and business partners, and I found peace in myself. No longer holding so many negative emotions in my body and my energy field, I realized I no longer needed antidepressants. Under doctor's supervision, I weaned off them.

I found the awakening process to be slow at times and fast and jarring at others. Like a knotted necklace, we take one knot at a time and work it, kneading it until the knot comes loose. In that area of our lives, the fog lifts and clarity appears. Where the knots do not release, the universe repeats the process until the last link in the chain unravels and is free.

Often when I finally got the message from a lesson, I realized just how many times the universe had presented me with circumstances that allowed me to see why that knot existed in the first place. When I reviewed my notes from my sessions with Susan, I realized how many times she had told me exactly how to detach and detangle. But until I did the real work, the knot remained, and the "Aha" moment was delayed.

Sometimes as we unearth our masterpiece, it doesn't look like we are achieving a lot on the earth plane. Yet what's happening on the outside may not reflect to the physical eye the real work being done on the internal spiritual plane. The foundation is being set and the way being cleared to be all that we can be as creator beings.

When I stepped back and looked at my own overall progress, I was pleased. Out of instinct, I looked up at the sky and asked God, "What do you think?"

7. Where Does Fear Still Rule Your Life?

This process made me realize just how many decisions in my life I had made that were based in fear. The fears we don't face become the chains that bind us. When we buy into them, they become patterns in our lives. If we can shift our patterns, we give the change we want a chance to manifest.

In all the unraveling, I was physically and mentally tired. I had asked my guides to show me to myself, and now I was asking them again to slow down. But it seemed I was so close to completing the cycle that my guides had one last push before pulling back. It no longer felt like fear was surfacing in small doses but in crashing waves. Night after night, I would wake up from awful dreams, lying in bed, swimming in doubt and anxiety, tormented by them. The fear welled up in me so greatly that the fear itself was uncomfortable. In my quest to eradicate fear and the habits that chained me to it, I actually started having conversations with my ego, saying, "You—get in the backseat and be quiet. If not, duct tape." I argued with fear saying, "You have no power over me. It is time for you to leave!"

Finally, the fear became so uncomfortable that I felt I had no choice but to let it go, to bust free like a bud ready to burst into flower. How painful the process of prying the heart open can feel, learning to trust, having courage to let go, and feeling like we are enough. For me it was not always a graceful process. I went kicking and screaming—scared. But it took just one moment for the initial release, and in that moment I let go of layer after layer of fear, judgment, lack, and limitation. Lying in the dark, I opened my eyes and told a sleeping world, "I no longer need your approval." I rolled over and went to sleep.

The next day I lay in bed, realizing I had passed the test. I felt the presence of White Eagle and understood he had come to celebrate the moment I surrendered my fight with fear and chose to love myself instead. I cried tears of sadness and tears of joy, understanding that a cycle in my life and soul's growth had ended. I had arrived home in a new way that day. I was free of many fears that had haunted me like ghosts of the people I had been.

Give Us This Day Our Daily Bread.

4

Step aside from all thinking,
And there is nowhere you can't go.
~ SENG-TS'AN, THE THIRD FOUNDING TEACHER OF ZEN

Creating in Love

AN IMAGE OF a beautifully wrapped package tied in gold ribbon formed in my mind's eye. I watched as someone pulled at the ribbon. Before I could tell who was untying it or what was inside the box, I was pulled from the dream. Now staring at the plaster design on the bedroom ceiling, I realized my cell phone was ringing.

I answered the phone to find Susan on the other end. As she started talking, it was clear that she was already aware of what had happened earlier in the week with my renouncement of fear. "When you first came to me, you were looking for ways to tap into the state of grace and manifest. But you were missing the connection with Spirit and using the material world as a benchmark for success. Having loosened the ego's grip, you now see yourself for who you truly are—unique, talented, and lovable. You have awakened to the power of faith, and you are more available to have a relationship with our loving and generous God. It's time to explore the beauty that is you—your inner power, your uniqueness, and the person you were meant to be," she said.

I was so grateful for Susan's help, and I was proud of the progress I had made. But as I hung up the phone, I felt a bit lost. While I was now aware of who I wasn't, I was still learning about who I really was and the process of creation itself. I was like a painter standing before a blank canvas, sorting through brushes and paints and deciding what to do with life's raw material. Like many who search for a calling and deeper meaning, I wondered—if I listen to my natural instincts, where am I to go? If life is about the expression of our soul or higher self, how do I best express my true nature? What am I to do? What can I create that continues to ripple positively beyond myself?

The future is simply infinite possibility waiting to happen.
What it waits on is human imagination
to crystallize its possibility.
~ Leland Kaiser

The Gift of Intention

Winter solstice was upon us, marking the shift in seasons and celebration of the return of the light. As it did each year, the cycling of the earth brought with it the celebration of the Christ child. The significance of the Christmas holiday had taken on a new meaning for me as I reflected on my own awakening and that of those around me. Beyond celebrating the birth of Jesus, it felt as if a new day was dawning in the consciousness of man—a time when we are born into a new understanding of ourselves and God's will for us. Woven into the rituals of the season are the reminders of our calling—illuminated candles, evergreen wreaths, and angels heralding, "Peace on Earth and goodwill toward all men."

As I walked across Susan's yard, ready to start the next phase of my growth, the sun was taking its final bow for the day. Daylight would soon be replaced with an endless display of twinkling stars. I was amazed how being in the country brought the night sky to life—a life that was dimmed by city lights and the "progressive" world we have created. Far from the hustle and bustle of the holiday season, there was a stillness that felt incredibly peaceful.

I melted into the landscape, feeling part of it, realizing how blessed I was to have found my teacher. I was filled with gratitude for the opportunity to learn how to be an expression of divine love in human form from a woman who celebrated Christmas every day.

Inside her cozy home, Susan began, as she had so many times before, to teach me. "As creator beings, visualizing and setting intention are how we create. Though we need ego, which operates from our head in order to create intent, we need to act on the intent with an open heart in order to complete our lessons and grow and evolve as souls. Every thought we think and every word we speak affirms what we believe to be true and what we intend for our path. Whether we understand it or not, actively or passively, our intentions have manifested all the current circumstances of our lives."

I looked down, reflecting on my current situation and where my ego-based thinking had gotten me this far. While I had made a lot of progress, I still had doubts.

Susan sensed what I was thinking and said reassuringly, "Don't tell me you can't; that isn't real. Instead move into the 'what if.' The question alone moves everything out of the way. Just by having that anchored in, we can do incredible things. Have absolute faith, and know that everything your heart truly desires will come. Remember this is not about making things fit but allowing the flow.

"Allow yourself to stop believing that struggling is the answer. As cocreators, what we focus on grows, so worrying only makes problems greater, and fear creates more fear. That is not what we want to be creating. Lack and limitation are born in fear, and fear is your ego trying to step back in to protect you. Tell your ego it's OK to accept the love and light that is flowing to you. It is the wind under your wings."

"This is where I get confused. Even though I understand that karmic loops come into play, it doesn't always seem as if life circumstances unfold as we intend," I said.

"The universe is always set up to give us exactly what we ask for," Susan replied. "When we introduce a new request into our vibration, it will be accepted or rejected, depending on whether or not it is in alignment with our beliefs and perceptions. It will sort through and add up all the pluses and minuses we put out there. What we receive is exactly what we ordered up.

"Those requests are intentions. Intentions are living energy—they are declarations we present to the universe about what we want to create," she added.

"Then intentions are different than 'will'?" I asked.

"Think about it this way. Intentions are meant to move the will in the same way programs give computers instructions; will is the computer, and intentions are the instructions."

As our conversation continued, I began to better understand the creation process. We harness the power of intention by using positive declarations like: "Abundance flows through every area of my life," "I am healthy, happy, and free from fear," and "I live in a state of joy—my life unfolds gracefully." We demonstrate our readiness for these intentions to come into our lives when we state them as if they are already taking place.

We then use creative visualization to add detail to the picture. We refine our requests and visualize what we want to create. We create images and stories in our heads, playing them out. We invent things without intimidation or self-consciousness. When we "act as if," we create the feeling that we have already received what we are asking for. And in doing so, we activate the vibration, and what we ask for is given to us.

"Creative visualization is something we use instinctively as children, but somewhere along the way our creativity goes underground, and we forget how to pretend. Many of us need to relearn this skill," Susan explained.

"Beyond that, the challenge most of us have with the process of creating is starting to notice what messages we put out there that contribute. We need to be conscious of what we unconsciously ask for, because we have forgotten that our thoughts and words have power. We also need to remember that for key things to take place, once we have declared an intention, we need to leave it alone and forget about the buts and hows and whys and whens," Susan said.

> *Universal substance is obedient to your conscious will at all times. It is constantly responding to humanity's thought and feeling, whether they realize it or not. There is no instant at which human beings are not giving this substance one quality or another, and it is only through the knowledge that the individual has conscious control and manipulation of a limitless sea of It that he begins to understand the possibilities of his own Creative Powers, and the responsibilities resting upon him in the use of his thought and feeling.*
> *~ St. Germain*

The Gift of Love

As our conversation continued, Susan shared, "Understand that intentions manifest based on the power behind them. *Love* is that positive force that helps us arrange creation."

As I listened, I was reminded how often Susan had told me to keep my heart open. I was starting to understand how much more that meant than just releasing fear and being kind. God's light, the Holy Spirit, is not just the breath of heaven that gives us life; it is the stuff life is made of. It is the pulsing, persisting raw material awaiting our artistic interpretation after the ego's trinity perception is cleared away. It is the energy of infinite love and unlimited possibility. The light of love takes many forms:

- Love is our inspiration.
- Love is the energy of healing and protection.
- Love is the mirror, showing us to ourselves.
- Love is our compass and our navigational system that helps us to find our path.
- Love is the energy behind our own buried treasures—our heart's desires.

- Love is the energy of manifestation we use to build and develop our lives.
- Love is the canvas and the expression of our unique talents and abilities.
- Love is the energy of giving and receiving and the unconditional example we are meant to follow.
- Love is our "daily bread."

God's Spirit is the streaming of light and the outpouring of love that is sent us moment by moment. It is the nourishing substance we depend on for life. God's love is so great that it is hard to fathom. In its purity, it is brighter than the midday sun, lighter than an evening breeze, more powerful than a hurricane, and more expansive than the known universe. It is not something we have to ask God for; it is not contingent on us doing or having anything. It is the gift we are given unconditionally; God expects nothing in return, and it is never rescinded.

When we pray, *"Give us this day our daily bread,"* we are asking God to provide us with the raw material—the light of love. We use that light energy to cocreate our lives, but we are not its pawns. We are both the catalyst for our life events and the "experiencers" of what we create.

When we let the light of Spirit flow through us, we tune into our higher self and God. Tuning in, we are more aware of our natural instincts and truths as spiritual beings. We become more aware of our divine path and the gifts we have been given to help us follow it. The level of understanding depends on the amount of light we allow to flow through us—or the degree to which our heart is open.

When I thought about love's light in terms of horsepower, the measurement for the potential power a car has, I started to see how important having an open heart is to cocreation. With a car, the greater the horsepower, the greater the car's potential for speed. In life, it is love that determines the potential to create; *love* is the eternal horsepower that fuels our intentions. But even though we ask God to provide that outpouring, *we* choose how much love we actually allow into our hearts by how negative or positive we choose to be and how many conditions we place on the circumstances of our lives. Like nature, we ebb and flow as we work to stay open and empowered, uncovering each aspect of our divinity.

In everyday life, we are like the sea anemone that contracts and expands in response to moderate changes in light intensity. We, too, expand and contract with the level of love and light energy we allow in our hearts. Where we no longer hold fear, our inner light is revealed. We open and tap into our creative power, and the life force within us accelerates.

Like the sea anemone, our hearts contract in response to darkness. When we allow fear and the ego's trinity perception to enter our lives, we loop back through the illusion. The life force within us decelerates, and our ability to create decreases. Where corners of darkness remain, our guides continue to show us our fracture and provide us with the opportunity to heal so we can move into our true power and master cocreation.

The expansion and contraction continues as we tackle life lessons. The more we keep our heart open through the trials and tribulations we face, the more love we are able to project. The more love we project, the more and faster we manifest. Elevating our consciousness, we vibrate higher and higher.

When we keep the channel fully open and reflect the light and love energy, we receive back into the world through our unique talents and gifts; we are on full throttle as Marianne Williamson explains in *Manifesting Abundance*:

> When we are at the height of our intellectual powers, of our emotional powers, of our psychological powers, there is an alignment of multi-dimensional energy systems [that] are within us that make up the human being. You get up in the morning, and you give that which is yours to give, what feels natural to give, that which is easy and effortless to give, that which gives you joy to give, and you are compensated by the universe in return.

When we are harmoniously aligned with the vibration of love, our personal power shines through in all its certainty. We cocreate lives of wholeness and holiness, maintain joy and peace in all situations, and share that grace with those around us.

But the choice is ours whether we give our power to something outside ourselves or operate out of our higher consciousness and use the raw material to create something divine.

Wherever your heart is, there you will find your treasure.
~ Paulo Coelho

The Gift of Purpose

THEN WHAT ARE we as individuals to create? Sorting through the information, it seemed as if there must be some greater meaning behind it for each of us. Would we randomly come here? And if we are each as unique as a fingerprint, what determines what attributes our soul is born into this life with?

Looking out the sunroom window at the starry night's sky, I asked, "Am I right in thinking that we all come here with a divine purpose?"

"Yes, everyone comes in with a purpose. For some, it may be to find peace within, find their own voice, or overcome fears. Others may have a mission that extends further beyond themselves—they may be called to be teachers, healers, or instruments of change. I have met some people whose soul's purpose was simply to have the experience. While some may not play a large role, we all have something to share, and we can all contribute to elevating our world," Susan said.

"But because we have free will, we determine if we will choose to live that out, right?" I asked.

"That's right. We determine what we are to accomplish in this life before we are born, but we are the copilots of this project, and we can steer it in any direction we choose—and even God doesn't know what path we will choose. Still, we are meant to be creating in alignment with the Holy Spirit, and God's light within us shines brightest when we are following our chosen life path. When we are making choices that help us accomplish the mission we chose for this life before we were born, his will and mine are one and the same—*thine*," she said smiling.

"When we choose to align with what we are meant to accomplish, the universe conspires to support us in its creation. Our angels and guides are working with us to adjust our view and help us see what we are supposed to be creating. They are guiding us to lives of healing and fulfillment of our contract. They are helping us see our divine purpose and be one with it. What we create helps our soul's growth and lifts everyone else up in the process."

Sorting through the information, I realized that these are missions we were built for. We were given abilities and even challenges to overcome in order to achieve them. Our mission really has nothing to do with mastering the material world. It is instead about being used as a vessel in which our will for our lives is the same as God's.

Our divine purpose opens our hearts in a way other things do not, accelerating our life force and helping us transcend. Like with Michelangelo, the sculpting doesn't end when we have chipped away enough to reveal the rough, raw form and figure. We spend time excavating to find our talents and gifts, adding detail to the masterpiece. We listen and follow the inner guidance that helps us identify them and what they truly mean in our lives.

We come into this life with a variety of things that make us shine. These gifts are not randomly generated or arbitrarily assigned. Our attributes—talents, gifts, and abilities—help us achieve our soul's mission. On some level, we all know that we will be called upon to use them. The key to understanding what they are and how God would have us use them is to look within and ask: What is it that comes naturally to me? What brings me joy—what do I love to do? What is it that fills me up in a way nothing else can? Answering these questions, we have a greater sense of what our higher self is trying to accomplish.

Finding our inner talents often awakens opportunities that have always been there but lay dormant, awaiting discovery. More importantly, once we understand what the talents are and how we are to use them, we realize how naturally life unfolds. Life has flow.

Looking past what the ego judges to be successful, we use our gifts to live on purpose. The unique and divine essence that has incarnated as our selves finds harmony and balance. When we do not understand what direction to take, we simply ask to be shown. Our natural talents, like diamonds in the rough, are revealed. For some, talents are easily identified, but others may have a hard time unearthing them—perhaps because their gifts and talents come as naturally as breathing or because fear still blocks them.

"Typically we come to this plane with more than one goal we hope to achieve. Each of our talents and gifts helps us to reach those goals. On a higher level, they come together in a highly integrated pattern of growth. For some of us, using them and living the life we are supposed to be living may mean stepping out of the life we are *currently* living," Susan added.

I could relate to that. "Well, I have already stepped way out of the life I thought I was supposed to live. The phoenix has been the symbol for my growth since before I met you; however, I was beginning to think the phoenix thought the ash was a bird bath," I said with a hint of sarcasm. "I really want to figure out what I am here to accomplish and move into it."

"The answer lies within you. Be still and listen to your heart. Let it be your compass," she said. "Pose the question to the universe, then step back and listen. Be receptive as new ideas form and resources are presented. They will be the stepping-stones that will lead you to your answer."

After my appointment, I drove through the countryside. The clear starry night had turned to a winter wonderland. Driving snow appeared out of the darkness in an unending shower of white that seemed to stream straight for my windshield. The wind gathered speed, and my headlights showcased the playful dance with waves of swirling snow. A world of possibilities was opening. And there was something else that arose from my heart, something I hadn't noticed before—a sense of longing to be used as a vessel.

I thought about my teacher and the life her higher self had chosen. Her calling was to serve as an intuitive healer and a counselor. When she started down this path, she was uncomfortable. But because she got past her fear and allowed herself to be guided, she had helped many people with everything from healing emotional wounds and physical ailments to manifesting their hearts' desires. She never advertised her services, but like with me, those needing help or seeking spiritual guidance seemed to find her. When I had asked her how that was possible, she explained that she had set the intention that those who were ready would be brought.

No, her path was not mine, but I was grateful for the example. I was ready to discover my soul's calling. I was ready to create my heart's intended song—the vibrational melody unique to me that longed to be expressed.

As I drove, my mind wondered, *Then what am I to do with my life, dear God? What is thy will and, therefore, mine? Yes, I can express an open heart where I am today, but I know there is more that you would have me create. What details shall I carve into my work of art in progress?* I drove on, taking in nature's show.

The next day, I felt guided to look to the *Pietà* for further inspiration. I started digging through books about Michelangelo and his masterpiece. I discovered that Michelangelo had been commissioned to create the statue. I learned that he was a deeply spiritual man who believed art was divinely inspired. His work represented a Neoplatonic philosophy—a belief that the truth and beauty of the spiritual world can be revealed through the physical world. Although he mastered a number of media as a painter, a poet, an architect, and an engineer, Michelangelo always considered himself to be first and foremost a sculptor.

I then turned to the *Pietà* itself and found picture after picture portraying its beauty from every angle. The statue had been my inspiration to peel back my life to reveal my true self, but as I read on my jaw dropped. I saw God at work through this statue in another way. The classic meaning of the word *Pietà* is "whole-souled abiding in divine will." Our purpose here on Earth is the same as the definition of the word *Pietà*—the statue's name!

I called Susan in my excitement to explain what I had found.

"Every time we leave something with a question mark, more information will come. When it comes, and we start linking it together, we will have moments so inspiring! Information is provided for us everywhere to help us on our journey. Some of it will be conscious, and some of it will be subconscious, but Spirit will present the information in a way that is relevant to us. Life experiences help us understand the information that is being brought, so be sure to stay open to the experience. The truth is that we learn from everyone who crosses our path. Even if we just meet a person for a moment, when they look us in the eye, they have information for us," Susan said.

"The information that I receive, I put back out into the world to help others so that when people sit quietly, they receive it. This information and what we create are meant to be shared. In truth, how can we contribute to the planet in a positive way if we don't experience the whole reason we came here in the first place?"

After our conversation, I continued my review of my raw material—what inspires me and what makes my heart soar. I meditated and listened. Peace washed over me as I realized that in my striving to get ahead, I had moved away from my love of writing, something that came naturally to me. I had done this because I didn't think I could excel in life as a writer in a way the external world found important. What messages along the way had made me think there wasn't value in that pursuit?

But I was getting the hint; God always has a plan for us and for our gifts. If we were not supposed to use them, they would not have been provided. If we are fearful about what the world thinks, even our natural talent will remain rough and unfinished. It is not up to the world to decide if our gifts have value anyway—God does not give questionable gifts, but have we stretched ourselves to use them?

Each of us can find our soul's purpose by using the tools we have learned. We meditate, we pray, and we set the intention to find our divine reason for being. We look within at what excites us. We search our hearts for what inspires us.

In my heart, I am a writer, enthralled with words. I love how words go from slim and curvy lines to sounds and syllables that paint a dream and jump off the page and into our hearts. I relish how words and phrases can be used to tell stories that move one to tears or to laughter. It was time to use this talent—not because it made me famous or wealthy, but because it opened my heart in a way other things did not. As Vincent Van Gogh once said, "Your profession is not what brings home your paycheck. Your profession is what you were put on Earth to do with such passion and such intensity that it becomes spiritual in calling."

To be a star you must shine your own light,
follow your own path and don't worry about darkness,
for that's when stars shine brightest.
~ Anonymous

The Gift of Inspiration

Then what am I to do with this gift? I wondered. *What am I to write about?* I searched for inspiration and the expression of my craft. Again, I meditated and prayed, and I let my mind wander. I allowed information to flow.

I started to see myself as the artist, silently creating my interpretation of life through art. I was a sculptor and a painter, and my canvas was life itself. I saw myself, the writer, coloring the canvas through words, describing in great detail the shifting light reflected in the world around me. I saw myself creating my own masterpiece, my own *Pietà*... the whole soul!

Like the master artist, I was inspired by the world. I could see God in the river that loudly rushes by and in the sprinkling of wildflowers swaying gently along its banks. I could sense his presence in the confident eagle soaring silently above. I could feel his profound love resonating through me, a love that neither fear nor death can destroy.

I am a soul participating in the Divine Mind, employing a body. In that body, I am a traveler regathering my truths. I am a mother and a daughter, a sister and a friend. I am a business owner and coach. I am a writer, a lover of music and books, and a student of spirituality and metaphysics. I am a work in progress of my soul's expression, creating my own room with a view. My work of art in progress is refined as I listen to the guidance of my heart.

As was so often true with other questions I had posed, the answers came in bits and pieces, and I was still not seeing the big picture. I knew all the pieces fit somewhere, but I was looking for the bridge that linked them together to reveal the answer to my question.

This new quest reminded me of twelve-hundred-piece puzzle I had done with my daughters. In the partially completed puzzle, the pieces that remained didn't seem to work together; the blue edge piece didn't seem important to the orange piece with three connecting points. We didn't see the relationship between the two until the piece that linked them together was discovered. The small, seemingly unimportant piece revealed that the blue and orange pieces were intimately connected—the blue piece was part of a peaceful sky, and the orange piece was a fall leaf hanging in the foreground. Once the interlocking puzzle piece was discovered, the puzzle came together perfectly to create a beautiful autumn scene.

In walking meditation, I allowed my inner voice to guide me. When I looked past what my physical eyes could see, I found that there was a piece of the puzzle around every corner. Each piece pointed to another and another. Pieces of information started to link together and formed awareness and understanding. I was amazed at the messages that pointed me down my path. I realized that for some time, they had been there, but my ego had created noise in the system that kept me from hearing, seeing, and recognizing that gut feeling that told me I was going the right direction.

I was just going about my day. But suddenly standing in the bathroom, brushing my teeth became a holy experience, and the answer came through loud and clear. I stared in the bathroom mirror. "Really?" I said. "Really? You want me to tell this story to the world?"

From a gentle place of knowing, I understood that I was provided with a gift and given a message to share with others. It was part of my path and purpose. Centered in my higher self away from chaos and fear, I was aware that I needed to let go at a greater level. I needed to let God guide me in the creation of a book.

I discussed what I had discovered with Susan in our next phone conversation. "I feel as if I'm supposed to write a book about my spiritual journey. Does that make sense?"

She paused, then sighed with newfound understanding, "Oh..." It seemed as if pieces of information for her had also now been linked. "I have wanted to find someone to help me explain what I understand. I have tried to write what I know, but I can't find the writer in me. I had asked that someone be brought to help."

Amazing! Susan's intention was to find a writer. My intention was to know myself and uncover my purpose. I couldn't help but wonder if this had been my destiny all along. I traced the energy line of my life curiously. Was I meant to be a student in this life so I could chronicle my unfolding to help others do the same?

In many ways the story was not just mine to tell. It is a message bigger than me and a bigger story reflected in mine. How many others have missed the master teacher's messages right in front of them that held the keys to life? Could I write a story that helps people understand the connections we miss and why? Could I explain the how-tos that had so helped me? I had to trust.

So my soul's work took a new path as I sat to write my journey to the center of myself. I gathered my notes and sat with pen in hand. I listened for guidance. I composed paragraphs and pages. Still the words remained disjointed fragments of the picture on a blurry horizon. Like the recesses of my mind, piles of lovely disconnected notes sat in the corners of my office. How do I pull a book from the bits and pieces became the new question.

> *Intention brings you the strength to arrange creation, and heart will guide your light so that your purpose shall be full of one's divinity shining like the moon reflecting the sun's intent to go on to stir the qualities that only heart can bring into blossom. The moon reflects the sun as our reality reflects our intention, and heart is what creates the fullness.*
> ~ Ra

Intention Backed by the Power of Love

The view from the sunroom window now displayed a snowy blanket. Outlines from the trees sketched shadows on the ground. Cheerful chirping echoed through the yard. Random chickadees shifted from tree to tree. As Susan sat down across from me, I turned my focus back to the sunroom and her. The sunlight reflecting off the snow lit the sunroom with a soft and embracing glow. "It may be my soul's calling—what it means for *my* soul to abide in God's will—but I am having trouble pulling information together into the form of a book," I said.

"The different aspects of intention are all important to the process. Our thoughts, our desires, our focus, and our faith are all important to the overall outcome. If we remove any one of them, the process loses its power. But when our thoughts, desires, and focus are in harmony, and we have absolute knowing that it shall be done, intention has the power to work miracles in our lives," she explained. Susan then walked me through the steps involved in manifesting abundance.

Step One: Open your heart.

"First, feel safe enough and open enough to let the love energy really flow. God speaks to us through an open heart. When we vibrate peace and work in conjunction with Spirit, manifestation is possible."

Step Two: Visualize and act as if.
"Second, visualize what you want to create. Picture in detail what you want, and focus on it with unwavering faith. Since your goal is to write a book, hold the picture in your mind and in your heart. Provide a great level of detail and be consistent so that what you bring is truly what you want. See it out in front of you, and pull it to yourself. Hold the book in your hands. See the image in great detail. Watch it go from a thought in your mind to something tangible. This is the essence of creation, where something appears where nothing was before. See the end result, and don't let anything move you from it," Susan explained.

"Also, act as if. Be excited about the change in front of you—excitement is creation energy in its purest form."

Susan told me a story of two women who both wanted to have a baby. They had both sought the help of doctors, but after trying several treatments, the doctors had given up on both of them. Feeling like they were running out of options, each contacted Susan. She gave both of them the same advice: "Hold that baby. Smell that baby as if it is already here. Do it over and over again until that baby is really lying in your arms."

The first woman followed Susan's instructions, visualizing and creating the feeling of excitement about the new life she wanted to bring into this world. The second told Susan she didn't want to do it, because if it didn't work, she would be disappointed. The first was soon pregnant and had a baby. The second did not.

As instructed, I held the picture in my mind and in my heart. I saw the book, looked at the cover, then turned it over and saw my picture on the back. I flipped the pages with my fingers. I held it as if it already was produced. My heart skipped a beat.

Step Three: Create a detailed picture of what you want.
"Be careful what you ask for. Be specific. The universe always brings you what you ask for," she continued. "For example, if you ask for a car when you really wanted a BMW, don't be upset when you get a beater.

"Also, be careful of what other messages you are putting out there that contribute to the picture. People may think that they are setting goals, wishing and hoping and praying for things that aren't being heard. But behind the scenes, every aspect is put into the equation. All doubt, all fear, and every 'I can't,' 'I don't deserve it,' 'It won't work,' 'I don't really believe' steers the boat in a different direction than we may think we are asking for.

"Understand the power we have to create. Our thoughts, words, and actions all carry energy and are powerful creating tools. Focus on need, and need grows. Focus on want, and want grows. If we don't ask, we get our answer anyway—more of the same. If we ask for something but do not have trust that it will appear, we cancel our request.

"All the positives and negatives contribute to the overall message we send about where we really want to go and what we really want to do and be in our lives. Whether subconsciously or consciously, each message contributes, and all the pluses and minuses add up to the coordinates of exactly where we are right now. Everything we put out counts, even comments we think mean very little like 'You're a pain in the neck,' or 'He's a loser.' And 'I don't deserve this' is very ugly energy. Turn it around. Always turn it around," Susan said.

Step Four: Start from where you are right now.

"It is also important to be OK with where we are right now and be open to the change we are asking for. We access the power of creation in the now.

"When we are OK with where we are, we can focus on life as we would have it be. We paint the picture and walk into it. If we are detailed enough about where we would like to go without too much attachment to how we get there, what we want to manifest will show up in our lives. But as long as we clutch anything—a rock, a person, or the past—our hands cannot be open to reach for something else. Our hands must be emptied before they can be filled anew. The same is true of our hearts and minds. Are they open or clenched shut?

"Appreciate in silence the life that is meeting you at every moment. Find gratitude for where you are right now. Gratitude not only helps us see the beauty in our imperfect perfection, it is the flint for creation. It ignites the process, starts the flow. When you are OK with where you are and have gratitude anchored in, your mind will be freed up to move into something new. Many people throughout history had a vision of something that others thought was not possible or told them was completely out of the question. But with the power of the mind aligned with pure intention, they changed the face of history."

Step Five: Don't be too attached to how you get there.
"Don't be too attached to how you get there. In truth, how can life be the orchestration of something grand, wonderful, and even bigger than we imagined if we stay attached to every aspect of how we receive what we have asked for? Doing so doesn't let the universe help us cocreate anything bigger than what the ego can imagine within the confines of our five-sensory experience. But if we see what we want, hold that picture in our mind and in our heart, and let life unfold, so much more is possible than we can even imagine."

Step Six: Claim it.
"And since this is a universe of vibration, nothing happens until something moves. Take a step and move the energy to get things started. In this way, we claim it. Take the steps needed to make your goals happen but with the intention that they will unfold easily and gracefully. In this case, get writing!

"What is supposed to happen flows naturally, but we do need to put some energy into it. Remember that if what you profess to want is *truly* what you want, there will always be energy there to make it happen," she explained.

Step Seven: Let go and let God.
"Now let go and allow your request to manifest. Once we have put the process in motion, we need to move out of our own way and allow things to unfold. It's like riding a bicycle built for two. God has the front seat, and we have the back. Because we are in the back, we don't always need

to pedal. We will make much more progress at this point if we take our feet off the pedals and enjoy the ride.

"And think about trying to steer from the backseat—it doesn't really work, does it? The same is true here. The minute we struggle, we shut down the process, because struggling is the attitude that *I have to do more to create*. When we do this, we are not letting energy come of its own accord. We need to really let go of life situations. We need to be detached but with the intent that it will all fall into place. If we don't create obstacles through struggling, we will always get what we need," she said.

"Like with all of God's laws, the laws of creation are demonstrated all around us. New shoots of life form under the soil's surface and then, in time, appear. From seeds, flowers bloom. From mere cells, embryos are formed that turn into babies and are born. Everywhere creation comes into being when an idea is formed and differentiated. In certain things, the results manifest quickly. In others, the process takes time and a lot of patience. Still, behind the scenes the universe is taking a dream and making it tangible. If we wait, it will appear. Every positive thought brings us one step closer.

"Give the universe room to work things out. Stay out of it enough that the universe can figure it out, because *you* can't figure it out."

As I reflected on the mechanics, I realized that for something to vibrate, we need to release it. For example, if we want to create a ringing sound using a glass and a fork, the noise doesn't happen until after we move the fork away. We allow the vibration of our intentions to be carried when we set the intent and then leave it alone.

Step Eight: Focus on it with unwavering faith.
"At this point, it becomes less about doing and more about being and trusting. It's about knowing with absolute faith that it shall be done. It doesn't take a whole lot of faith either—we just need to find faith the size of a mustard seed to be able to transform our lives. All we need to do is grab on, hold it, and anchor it as truth. We don't need a lot, but keep in mind that with greater faith comes greater creative energy."

Step Nine: Patiently watch for the stepping-stones.
"Remember that at this point all the pieces will be up in the air. You don't know how to get where you want to go from here. Step back and let the universe set it up so that all the pieces of the puzzle come back together differently, more in line with what you truly want. Let it come more in line with your higher self and why you came here in the first place. Trust and go with the flow.

"Most people would think that focus means determination. But it really has less to do with determination than it does with observation. And observation is all about watching for the opportunities the universe sends us that meet our intention. Put the pictures out there, and the universe will provide you with some pretty big how-tos.

"Stay open to possibilities. Let God handle it, and pay attention. Have great faith that whatever you need will come as you follow your path. And remember that when your energy is amped up, big leaps and great synchronicities happen.

"Feel the energy, and watch for the stepping-stones. What others dismiss could have incredible value—be open-minded. Let Spirit be your guide. Let it flow, and pay attention. We might come up with a solution to a problem we've been focused on when we sleep or when we are out and about in life."

Step Ten: Allow the change, and know that you are worthy.
"Then stay out of your own way and allow the change to happen. For many of us, manifesting comes down to feeling like we deserve what we want and feeling comfortable with the shift the manifestation will create in our lives. Allowing ourselves to know we are worthy goes back to the ego's trinity perception.

"Be aware that the ego would keep us in want and the idea that we are not enough keeps us from our greatness. Ask yourself what obstacles you are creating that keep you from going where you need to go. Believe you are worthy, or your order will be cancelled," Susan said.

"Stay anchored in the knowledge that you are enough and do deserve your heart's desire, in this case, a completed and published manuscript and career as an author."

Step Eleven: More, please!
"When things start showing up in your life, support that vision by saying 'More, please.' If the option that appears isn't what you thought you ordered, adjust the request and the picture you hold in your mind.

"Allow life to unfold, and know that what we receive is given to us to show us to ourselves and help us grow who we are. Know that what we receive is useful, even if it doesn't seem to make sense to us. If we judge what is brought, we find ourselves in a state of contraction. If we look at it as good or bad, we slow or even stop the flow. Remember the tighter the grasp, the less the flow. Trust that what is brought is a gift, whatever it is. If we trust God with our eternity, we can trust him with our present. There is always a greater orchestration beyond what we understand," she went on.

Miracle-Minded Thinking
"Remember that the world beyond the five-sensory logic is where unlimited potential lies. But keep in mind that that also means not looking to the ego self for the direction life should take. It means listening and acting from our heart and letting it be our guide, using intuition and not intellect to create our lives. When we do this, a vast system is there to support our growth and happiness. When we master intent, all the forces of the universe can align to make what seems impossible possible."

Thinking it through, I realized it isn't always easy for people to let go at this level and trust. We are conditioned by the physical world to think we are limited. We are like the elephants in the circus. Circus elephants are chained to stakes from the time they are little and are not able to roam outside a confined space. While they may try and pull away when they are young, over time, the elephants become less resistant, accepting imposed limitations as their own. They are so conditioned to believe they cannot move outside the confined space that, even after they grow into enormous animals, they are tethered by merely a thin rope. They accept the imposed limitations even though they are strong enough to pull the entire circus tent over.

"Each of us is chained to the illusion until something changes our minds and demonstrates the power we have to manifest and heal just as Jesus did. But when we connect with Spirit and work in meditation and gain clarity, the power of intention and visualization take on new life—the higher our vibration, the greater our understanding of the universe and our role in it. The greater our knowing, the more we understand that intention is the center of the evolutionary process—it is the engine of evolution," Susan said.

I was trying to pull this new information together with the pieces I already had, but the blended weave still had many frayed edges. Jesus. Peace. Spirit. Love. Creation. Thy will. Jesus. Peace...

Seeing the cogs in my thinking, Susan offered, "Try looking at Jesus's teachings in the context of metaphysical Christ consciousness. Life will take on a whole new meaning."

With that, the light bulb turned on! It wasn't until then that the pieces started to come together in a *much* greater picture. What I hadn't grasped until that point was that Susan was teaching me more than how to find peace and heal my life. She was teaching me about quantum physics, sacred geometry, and the energy field that connects man and matter and continually affects everything and everyone!

Looking back, my fascination with metaphysics had helped me find spirituality and an understanding and connection with God. Spirituality led me to Jesus and the Christ consciousness. Studying Jesus's teachings led me back to metaphysics and quantum physics. The Christ consciousness had brought me to a converging point between science, religion, and spirituality. The Christ consciousness explains everything from gravity and electromagnetism to superhuman gifts, including instantaneous manifestation, telepathic communication, clairvoyance, and spontaneous healing. Everything we consider miraculous can be traced back to quantum physics.

What I found even more fascinating about all of this is how often we silo information, not seeing that religion and spirituality are variations on a theme or how science and spirituality are different ways of explaining the very same concepts. But often, to see the relationship between them, we need to open to the metaphysical aspects woven through the religious and spiritual stories and references.

From God's perspective, surely the distinction is unimportant, but for humans who have been taught to trust what is scientifically proven, it is game changing.

Einstein proposed that we live in a quantum universe, one built out of tiny, discrete chunks of energy and matter. At the same time, Max Planck, a physicist from Berlin and the father of quantum theory, discovered that everything in the universe, including our bodies, is connected to and interacts through a field of energy. This field, often referred to as the Zero Point Field, contains the blueprint for our existence; all information from all of time is said to be stored there. Our interaction with the field determines who we are, who we will become, and who we have been.

Planck's research described the smallest particles in the universe and found that they vary between two states: waves and particles. The energetic dance between these two states shifts and conforms to our beliefs, judgments, and expectations and creates matter—or what we call life. When we watch something, it is our conscious observation combined with our belief system that locks a possibility into place as our reality. In other words, science has proven that our thoughts do create our world! This in turn confirms we are indeed cocreators of our lives and not passive observers.

In his book *The Divine Matrix*, Gregg Braden draws analogies to help us understand the concept of quantum physics. Braden describes how a movie theater projects a moving image on a theater screen. The movie is really just many still pictures being flashed very quickly one after another. Even though we know that the image is an illusion, our brain merges the images into what we perceive to be uninterrupted movement. He states that quantum physicists believe our world works in much the same way. Braden explains:

> The expectation or belief we hold while we are observing is the ingredient in the soup that chooses which possibility becomes our 'real' experience. In other words, faith becomes a

key component. When we believe that our desires will be fulfilled, our world inevitably conforms to that assumption.

Making the connection, I realized that it's the Zero Point Field that we tap into for information and receive answers to the questions we ask.

"I call it the universal library," Susan explained. "It is the place where all information is stored. Ask the right question and be tapped in, and another door is opened. I see the ego self, actually, as a computer virus that scrambles the messages. Our lives are all about unscrambling the messages and regathering our truths.

"Once we see that *we* cocreate our own reality, we realize that we have the power to change that reality into anything we truly desire. And Jesus came to show us," Susan added.

Jesus demonstrated the potential we all have. He was a shining example of how to live in order to fulfill our soul's calling. He knew that despite how dark the world may look, God is always present. He understood the power of Spirit and that through Spirit we can bring what we deeply believe into our reality. Because of this, he was able to produce what many consider to be miracles. But Jesus said, "These things I do, you can do and more," expressing that we all have the power and potential he demonstrated if we integrate this knowledge into our lives.

In *The Consciousness of The Christ: Reclaiming Jesus for a New Humanity*, Kell Kearns describes what Susan had shared:

> When he got into the boat his disciples followed him. And, behold there arose a great storm in the sea, so that the boat was covered with the waves; but he himself was asleep. And, they came to him and awoke him saying, "Save us, Lord. We are perishing!" And he said to them, "Why are you timid, you men of little faith." Then, he arose and rebuked the wind and the sea; and it became perfectly calm. And the men marveled saying, "What kind of man is this, that even the winds and sea obey him?" Jesus is saying, "You could have taken care of this yourself! Calm comes from peace, not fear, and there is peace abundant in you. Be conscious. Do not be swept away by waves that belie

your true nature. Be as gods. For this you were created. Be peace and tranquility and storms shall end. Your faith, fully realized, can move mountains. Excuse me now, I'll get back to my nap."

"As we grow as souls, we learn to see beyond the five-sensory world and what the ego would have us believe to be real. We begin to understand that we too are the vessel for God's expression and that *'The Father within doeth the work.'* As we grow in understanding of universal principles and metaphysical laws, we understand our ability to master them as Jesus did. We know that if we believe something and have absolute faith, it will happen. Jesus often said that, 'It is done unto you as you believe.' Like Jesus, we express gratitude for the good we know will follow because we know that our prayers are always answered," Susan explained.

"Incredible! So we all have access to all information and can create anything we want if we tap into that energy field. Then, truly, it is only the stories that we tell ourselves about what life is about that keep us locked into a five-sensory experience!" I said.

"There are limitless possibilities in life if you are open to them and allow them to happen, and it doesn't always come down to 'doing.' Nor is it about mine versus yours and who gets there first. We are often taught there are only so many pieces of the pie, and that is not true. Winning and losing is ego-based thinking. From the perspective of Christ consciousness, there are infinite possibilities for creation and plenty for everyone. Remember that the realm of the miraculous is us asking the Divine Mind what *it* wants and not just trying to raise our standard of living."

"Then the Christ consciousness helps us understand that we have the ability to create miracles—to be a channel for them," I responded.

Smiling, she added, "Now you see that you've had the ruby slippers all along."

My life was being transformed with this knowledge! I realized I could grasp the information within a book simply by holding it. If I couldn't find something or remember where it was, I reminded myself that I already knew the answer, and I waited for it to come to me. When

I allowed myself to believe it, it did. Amazing—every nutrient our body needs, everything we need to heal emotionally, physically, and spiritually, and literally every piece of knowledge is at our fingertips if we trust and tap into it. We can use it to create our reality. There is one small catch, though...

In *The Divine Matrix,* Gregg Braden explains that it is important that we remember the purity of thought behind our request that helps us manifest. In terms of cocreating our life circumstances, Jesus said, "Ask and you shall receive." But we must ask without hidden motive or attachment to the outcome. We make requests from the clarity of Spirit and not from the judgment of the ego's trinity perception. It is the state of being we are in that calls the blessing forth, rather than something that we do.

Braden also explains that ancient prayers that were recorded in Aramaic have recently been retranslated. The new translations demonstrate how "tremendous liberties were taken over the centuries with the ancient authors' words and intent." For example, John 14:13-14 in the modern and condensed King James Version of the Bible reads:

> Whatsoever ye ask the Father in my name, He will give to you. Hitherto have ye asked nothing in my name: Ask and ye shall receive, that your joy may be full.

Compare this with the original text (recent retranslation) that reads:

> All things that you ask straightly, directly...from inside My name—you will be given. So far you haven't done this...So ask without hidden motive and be surrounded by your answer—be enveloped by what you desire, that your gladness be full.

In other words, we must ask with an open heart.

What it came down to now was learning to use the concepts in my own life as they were presented. *Knowing how much more is possible,* I wondered, *what more do I create? How can I contribute to our world?*

How do I proceed in the fulfillment of my divine purpose in the spirit of surrender, without judgment or ego expectation?

Meditating on my new goal, I realized that my purpose dictated my direction now. Beyond the need to focus and create a story, there were other things to consider. If I was really going to focus on writing a book, I would need help to financially stay afloat, raise my kids, and undertake what I now understood to be part of my soul's calling.

Because we had worked to maintain and heal our relationship, my ex-husband, Carl, and I talked it over. We decided that I would move back in and work on my project, and we would see if we could work things out between us. It was certainly an unconventional decision, but in my life of surrender, there seemed to be many of those. Yet, doing this would give me a chance to write with less financial worries and see if that spark was still there.

You'll see it when you believe it.
~ Wayne Dwyer

The Gifts of Cocreation
Once the girls and I had moved back in and all the boxes were unpacked, I sat in my old office, writing. I started to witness my intentions become tangible. Before that time, this book had been a huge stack of notes from my sessions with Susan, but when I began using the power of intention, the book started to take form.

I reflected on quantum physics and the concept of cocreation. I realized that when Michelangelo said, "I saw the angel in the marble and carved until I set him free," he was talking about this very process. He held the image of what he wanted to create in his mind and was guided to create it. Einstein, Edison, Disney, Ben Franklin, and so many others practiced the power of intention and quantum physics and created what was impossible before. Since the creative genius within me is equal to the creative genius within you is equal to the creative genius in Einstein and Disney or anyone who chooses to challenge ego-imposed boundaries, we too can create amazing things. In a whole new way, I understood that we are the variable.

I was reminded about how my striving to make life happen a certain way got me nowhere. But, our heart's desires—approached with the power of intention and combined with movement in the right direction, a smidgeon of passion, and a small amount of faith—can move mountains and at incredible speed. I found that Spirit fed me the energy and the information and provided the stepping-stones to my new goals, but only if my mind was clear enough, I noticed, and could act on, the infinite supply of energy that flowed. Where things didn't flow, I understood that I was the one that closed the aperture, or it was not the path I was supposed to take—there simply was no energy trail to follow.

The concepts again are not all that hard to comprehend, but one does need to put them into practice. Through my business, I had learned to create goal and vision statements. I knew I needed to have the picture of what I wanted in place before it would actually be possible. I found having a journal and writing out my intent with enough clear detail about what I wanted helped me define that direction. But less and less, I felt the need to fill in the "how-tos." I worked to keep my heart open and free of doubt and fear and moved in the direction of my intention, but I left the rest to the universe.

As time went by, I saw the power of intention and quantum physics at work in other people's lives around me. Amazing things started to happen as I watched others use this knowledge. My friend Sarah received a $10,000 check from Santa Claus just when she thought she might lose her home. My friend Katie's whole financial situation seemed to change for the better within the course of a week. Incredible miraculous things! In my own life, business contacts appeared, and I landed another contract position. I reached out to several authors and heard back from many of them. They were open to providing guidance and helping me make contact with agents and editors. Had I not gone through this process, I never would have thought that was possible.

The law of attraction and the power of intention were clearly demonstrated in another way. My daughters and I had been invited to Minnesota to spend time with my sister and her family. But I didn't know how I would manage it financially. A stone had recently hit the windshield of my car, and as winter temperatures plummeted, the small chip started to radiate and spread, developing into what looked like a beautiful growing snow crystal. On top of the problem with the windshield, my car was in desperate need of new brakes.

Though I had never stated it out loud, I wondered how I would have the repairs done and still be able to afford the trip. I really didn't feel it was safe to make the trip like this with my kids in the car. The date was fast approaching. I didn't change my plans; instead I remained open, looking for the answer.

One morning soon after we had been invited to the Twin Cities, I drove in to a neighboring city where I was doing contract work. I found myself sharing the road with a woman driving an Audi who was obviously in a hurry. Weaving in and out of traffic, she started tailgating me. Not interested in being knocked off my positive attitude, I moved over to the left lane and let her pass me by. As I moved over, she flew by me. But somehow as we drove into town, we ended up next to each other once again.

We drove through a roundabout side-by-side—I was in the left lane, and she was in the right. As we came around to the other side of the roundabout, I went straight and she turned left, steering her car into the front end of my car. We weren't going fast, but we now had come to a grinding halt in the middle of the intersection. Crunch!

I anchored in peace and exited my car to assess the damage. The woman opened her car door. Staying seated, she proceeded to yell at me, shouting not so nicely about how she did this same thing every day, and the accident was my fault. I calmly smiled. (Inside I thought, *You don't get to take my personal power*.) I introduced myself and explained that it might be a good idea if we moved our cars to a store parking lot just past the roundabout. Still upset and ranting, she slammed her door shut and drove into the lot.

After parking a few stalls away, I called the police to report the accident. I stepped out of my car to get a closer look at the damage. The front corner of my car now looked like crumpled tinfoil someone had tried to smooth out. Beyond that, I was going to be late for work and wondered how I would now make the trip to Minnesota. I did my best to keep my cool as I sat in my car waiting.

When the policeman arrived, he spent over an hour with the woman trying to get her to understand that roundabouts are not designed to make left turns from the right lane and that the accident had, indeed, been her fault. After the lengthy debate, the policeman came to my car, apologized for the wait, and explained the situation. I was given an accident report number so that I could contact the woman's insurance company to have the damage to my car assessed and repaired.

Once I did, I saw the power of intention at work. The insurance rep informed me that the body shop needed to order parts, and it would take two to three weeks to get them in. The rep offered me a rental car to use until mine was fixed and said he would keep me updated. The rental car was my answer I had nonverbally asked for! What had seemed like a negative situation was actually a blessing! I was able to drive it to Minnesota, compliments of the ranting woman, and it bought me time to pay for the other car expenses when commission checks I was expecting came in.

As crazy as it may sound, I was so grateful for this accident. It had demonstrated the creation process. This greater understanding changed my perception, and, because of it, my whole approach. It was no longer just about pulling something to me that I currently didn't have but showing up in my day-to-day life and giving to life what best I could with joy and a sense of commitment. It was about *being* different in my life; it was about bringing a sense of reverence to it—physically, emotionally, spiritually. Less afraid, I found joy in a state of being. I found satisfaction in the small tasks in front of me. I gave to life what before I expected life to give to me. It was done without expectation of return. It was done in gratitude for what I realized I had already been given.

When one tugs at a single thing in Nature, he finds it attached to the rest of the world.
~ John Muir

The Gift of Connectedness

Science has demonstrated that at the quantum particle level, there's something within each of us that isn't limited by time, space, life experiences, or even death. Quantum physics also demonstrates what Susan had already shared with me and what the mystics have been saying throughout the ages—we are all connected.

My guides showed me a picture with rows of people holding hands. At times it seemed like the line gently swayed back and forth. Other times the row looked like a tug-of-war. I gathered that the line represented etheric chords that exist between people, between people and objects, and between people and places. Note that I use the term *chord* and not *cord*, because my understanding is that they are harmonic and resonant in nature.

This phenomenon is explained through another quantum theory called entanglement. Entanglement is so weird that Einstein dubbed it "spooky action at a distance." This theory states that where an object becomes entangled with another, an action performed on one will affect the other—even if the two entangled objects are separated by large distances.

Everything we see, everything we touch creates a thread of energy between ourselves and it. These chords are the underlying nature of how relationships connect people. Like "apron strings" between mother and child, chords are how we exchange empathy, love, and information. This exchange happens on an unconscious level for most people.

Energy flows back and forth through these chords, into and out of our chakras. Through these chords, energy can be discerned, pumped into, or drained away from another person without his or her knowledge.

We all have chords attached to other people, and, for the most part, we don't need to concern ourselves with them, because they connect us to people who love and support us. Through them, we feel the ebb and flow of life; the more open we become, the more we feel the shifts of the collective thought and consciousness in our neighborhoods, our communities, our countries, and across the globe. The chords that bind us with love remain permanently embedded in our energy system.

Negative chords are released or cut. (The process of cutting chords is explained in chapter 5.)

More and more I became aware of these connections. One week I found that I was unable to sleep—almost not at all. Night after night, I laid awake with strange feelings of anxiety around different people in my life. I felt a shift happening but was unaware of what it represented. The feeling seemed to whisper of change.

I was anxious. I reached out to the people around whom I felt the intense anxiety. In conversation after conversation, I found out that none of my feelings were a coincidence. That during this time, the earth-ties between us had shifted as people in our lives decided to journey home. While I felt that each had gone to a wondrous place, their absence felt like sinkholes, even though I'd only experienced a "relationship" with them through my ties with others. It was as if I was standing on the edge of a crater, holding onto others who were emotionally pulled into an energy gap. Amazing. How interconnected we really all are!

Each of these souls were and are important cogs in the wheels of my family: a four-month-old from halfway across the world that my niece and her husband were supposed to adopt but who had died of malaria; a beloved friend of my brother-in-law who decided to take his life; and the cherished father of my sister-in-law whose mission in life was complete.

I had a deepening awareness of the shifts, even though none of them were with people I knew well or even directly. Those shifts felt beautiful, yet bittersweet. I felt compassion for the people who had been left behind and peace for those who had passed on. I felt our oneness. It reminded me of the value of each person we are connected to in the web of our life and how that shift really does affect each of us whether we are aware of it or not. It was beautiful to experience open hearts reaching out to open hearts that otherwise might appear to be closed.

The blessing of each other and our connectedness is an incredible gift, and yet so often we overlook it completely. So often we are so focused on ourselves that we miss the value of giving *and* receiving and allowing the flow of positive energy between us. We miss the importance of reestablishing our wholeness and working toward our collective purpose: creating peace on Earth.

We make a living by what we get,
but we make a life by what we give.
~ Winston Churchill

Sharing Our Gifts
Spirit energy is meant to be shared. In sharing, we can help others heal—whether it helps them relieve physical or emotional pain, find their paths and their truths, or produce a world of abundance. Every relationship is an opportunity to share, and sharing our gifts brings us closer to becoming unified in our humanity, living in peace.

We all come to the table with different spiritual gifts, whether we are teachers, healers, or communicators sharing information. These gifts are like different pieces of the universal puzzle. We learn where each piece goes and how to use it to find our own truths. But the assembly process doesn't stop there. Our little corner of the puzzle only makes sense when we share and help others understand where their puzzle pieces go. In this way, every kindness we extend to another is a blessing unto ourselves.

Developing and sharing our authentic selves is the driving force that brings us here, adding to the beauty of this world through our blessings and not taking from it. Coded deep within each of us is the desire to let love flow through us and share it freely out in the world; it is our instinctive nature to be humane beings, not focused on competition but on supporting the goal of the harmonious unity of all.

The concept was demonstrated on a small scale very clearly for me. My daughters, nine and twelve, got silly bands for St. Nicholas Day. Silly bands were popular at the time; they were shaped and colored rubber bands that kids wore on their wrists and traded with their friends. Each daughter got a different package—one received silly bands shaped like animals such as rabbits, wolves, and walruses. The other got a fantasy-themed assortment that included fairies, unicorns, mermaids, and phoenixes. After the girls pulled them from their Christmas stockings, my younger daughter started eyeing up her sister's pile and said, "I like yours. I want that one and, oh! I need that one."

I interjected, "You each got different packs so you could share." That was an 'Aha' moment for me. We all have received different gifts from God so that we can learn to share. Life is about learning to open to love and share what we have received. It is not about displaying our gifts for others to see and admire. God is truly after the heart of the willing giver and an open receiver. We are all given opportunities to bless each other and, at the same time, allow God to do amazing things in our lives. In essence, we are given each other to help us open our hearts and expand our view.

Many of us put that sharing on hold in order to accumulate, but if we pay attention and are truly present, we realize that every day God sends us someone for whom we hold a gift—and in fact, every person and every thing that comes to us provides us an opportunity to share something and share it unconditionally. We must simply be open to the experience in order to learn what it is.

All of life becomes an opportunity to uncover and develop our unique talents and gifts and to express them in love and light without any expectation of return. Your gifts and mine may be different, or they may be the same, but by virtue of the fact that they are given to us, we know that they are to be reflected out into the world for the betterment of all.

When we grasp what God would have us do with our resources, talents, gifts, and creations, we don't find ourselves money rich and relationship poor, collecting people and relationships, but unhealthy and unhappy or totally in fear that someone will take what we have created. But if we let the ego self step in and make decisions based on something outside ourselves, we miss our God-given opportunity to shine and raise each other up.

We open ourselves to giving and receiving, knowing each person is exactly where they are supposed to be in life. When we do this, we allow them the opportunity to grow just as we are growing. We learn to give and receive regardless of whether the other person has learned to give and receive yet or not. We acknowledge our own gifts, and we acknowledge those of others without judgment.

When we change our perspective from self-centered ambition to love-centered service, we find our path opens up to us. Shifting our focus back to gratitude, joy, and positive intentions, we will find that abundance flows and expands in countless directions beyond what the ego would tell us defines life's canvas. We move beyond the need to control or be perceived as powerful to the physical world. Instead, we reflect the power within in all its certainty, and we see that we are already abundant beings on many more levels than we understood. We benefit all of humanity and creation, not just ourselves.

As we move from the ego's trinity perception to becoming creator beings, we move from inner focused to miracle minded. We change our minds about who we are and our purpose on Earth, and express our true beingness out in the world. When we live from our higher self, and use the power of love as it's intended, the gift of life is unwrapped.

And Forgive Us Our
Trespasses,
As We Forgive Those Who
Trespass Against Us.

5

I invite you to enter the dance without taking yourself too seriously. None of you are professional dancers. But every one of you is capable of learning the steps. When you step on someone else's toe, a simple "sorry" will do fine. You are all learning at the same time and mistakes are to be expected.
~ PAUL FERRINI

Releasing and Letting Go
I WOVE IN AND out of puddles as I made my way to the farmhouse. I stopped purposely, yet playfully, to break up one of the remaining patches of snow that glistened in the midday sun. A robin landed on a branch along the yard, cheerfully announcing his return, singing a cappella with an unseen chorus. Everywhere tiny shoots were emerging, shifting the scenery from winter white to luscious green. Acting in concert, nature shared its emerging beauty.

Susan was waiting for me at the door and welcomed me. As we made our way through the house, she shared that her circumstances had changed. She was in the process of looking for an apartment and would soon be moving. She wasn't attached to material things, so downsizing wasn't something that bothered her. It was more a process of figuring out what to get rid of and how.

As I listened, I thought about what the shift would mean for her. The farm had been her sanctuary. Putting myself in her position, I empathized. Leaving it would be hard—much less the work it takes to move. I glanced around. My eyes passed over and then returned to the wooden "Pietà" sitting on her shelf. For a moment I didn't feel I could ask, but I knew if I didn't, I would never know. Finally, pointing to it, I said, "I would buy the statue from you."

Susan looked at me and smiled. "Sure."

After my appointment, I left with my new treasure. When I was home again, I set the statue on the dining room table. I dug through my shelves, looking for a book on Renaissance art. I flipped through the pages until I spotted Michelangelo's *Pietà*. I studied the picture curiously, comparing it to the statue in front of me.

With Michelangelo's statue, Mary cradles the lifeless body of Jesus after he was taken down from the cross. Her face is peaceful as she looks down at her son. There is no anger or blame in her expression, even at a time when one would think she would be ravished with fear, judgment, and hatred. Jesus's body conforms to hers, portraying their closeness. His face is serene. The scene does not portray any harshness, only love and tenderness.

I compared the picture in the book to the wooden statue sitting in front of me. The statue Susan had found closely resembled Michelangelo's, but it was different. The stabilizing figure was Jesus. There was a horseshoe-shaped crack that formed his mantle, and the grain in the wood clearly detailed his facial features, including his beard. From the back, it looked as if he was cradling a human heart. From the front, Jesus appeared to be holding someone, perhaps a child, representing humanity and the communion between man and God sanctified through Christ. The same love and acceptance was detailed in the form and grain of the wood that Michelangelo had carved into quarried marble.

This piece of wood held so many messages. How brilliant to use the *Pietà* to deliver answers and confirm understanding—a wooden statue no less, a sign from the carpenter himself. Glancing past the statue, I fell deep in thought. As powerful as he, so are we. Then we must find the same compassion, understanding, and forgiveness that Jesus did. Looking at the pure expressions depicted in each statue, that seemed a tall order to fill. I was humbled by the incredible compassion and forgiveness. As loving as he, can we be?

I reflected on my own life. I had made progress. I had let go of a lot in my continued effort to free my own heart. New situations highlighted ongoing challenges, and, now that a path had been cleared, deeply buried issues found their way to the surface—things I hadn't realized I was hanging on to. Living with Carl again certainly accentuated some of them. The difference was that now I saw the issues that came up as an opportunity to heal and grow; I was aware freedom from fear couldn't completely happen until I unlocked the doors to forgiveness for myself and those around me.

I remembered Susan saying that love mirrors for us everything unlike itself—anything unloving, anything that is not God-like—so it can be released. Where we still have unresolved issues, emotional triggers bring them back around so they can be healed. Looking again at the carpenter's "Pietà," I realized that forgiveness is that release. It is the process of releasing karmic energy that heals us spiritually, mentally, and emotionally. It frees us from the ties that negatively bind us, and, as such, our energy rises.

As we interact with others and the world around us, we share, grow, and elevate our consciousness. Emotional triggers show us where we still need to heal; suffering shows us the crosses we still bear. Through forgiveness, we loosen the chords that bind us to those we feel have hurt us. In widening circles in the web of life, we remove the walls that appear to separate us. The peace we have found within becomes the basis for harmonious relationships with all of God's creation. Reaching past the illusion, we blend and harmonize in a united rhythm and frequency.

Still, as I gazed at the statue, I wondered...

It is not more surprising to be born twice than once;
everything in nature is resurrection.
~ Voltaire

Rebirth

It was my last visit to the farm. I followed Susan through her kitchen and living room, weaving through packed boxes and noticing the unseen shifts that come from change. We entered the sunroom and sat down. After exchanging small talk, I broached the topic of Jesus's crucifixion. "Did Jesus really die that horrible death?"

"Yes. Yes, he did," she said.

"But he was capable of miracles. He could have stopped it. Why did he let that happen?" I asked.

"Jesus knew it was going to take place. He even told his disciples it needed to take place, because he was going to show them something," she responded.

"The resurrection?"

"Yes, the transcending—his coming back. But that message was corrupted. Pontius Pilate put him on a pedestal so that the masses wouldn't understand their own power. But Jesus clearly included everyone when he said, 'You will do these things also.'"

"Even in a horrible situation, he thought of others before himself," I responded, better understanding the significance of his actions.

"His words from the cross were, 'Father, forgive them; for they know not what they do,'" she replied.

"Through his actions, he showed us the incredible depth of forgiveness," I said, realizing that Jesus demonstrated the power we all have to handle any adversity. If we are to follow that example, we move from a life of fear and judgment, even in what seems to be horrific circumstances, to a place of peace and healing. We look at and acknowledge the pain but do not dwell on it. We instead remember who we are underneath and why we came here; we move through and release any blocks, becoming more and more a perfect expression of divine love.

"Of everything Jesus demonstrated for us, forgiveness seems the most profound. How do we follow that example?" I asked.

"Forgiveness is often hard for people, because they don't grasp reincarnation. We have discussed karma already, and karma and reincarnation go hand in hand. While karma means accountability, reincarnation is another word for opportunity. Together they help us understand how we got where we are and what we do about it," she explained.

Seeing the doubt on my face, Susan reassured me, "While these concepts are often not taught today, both karma and reincarnation were taught by Jesus."

Still I hesitated.

"Think about it. How many of us have déjà vu moments? How many of us meet a person that we are instantly repelled by or instantly drawn to? We may look at people around us today and not know why we have issues with them, but we feel the emotion.

"Many times we don't know why we feel something or what motivates us to act in certain ways. Tracing energy lines back and asking where they are coming from may not always result in an answer if we are only looking through this lifetime and thinking that this is our only incarnation. We may have to look back many lifetimes and through our ancestry to uncover the source of an issue," she said.

I had often wondered about reincarnation. I've even done past-life regressions to see what I might learn. I was curious, but I hesitated to take it too seriously, because I understood the concept to be incompatible with Christianity. The message that reincarnation is just a myth had been deeply planted in my brain.

Susan explained that if we look back, we see that the early Christian church taught about reincarnation. Those early teachings were centered in the understanding that God was the source of the soul, and the soul's journey back to oneness with God happened through many incarnations. In those teachings, salvation was not linked to a person's relationship with the church but to his direct relationship with God. But about five hundred years later, all that changed. In order to have full power and authority over Rome, Emperor Justinian (c. 482–565) forced the ruling cardinals to draft a papal decree stating that anyone who believes that souls come from and return to God would be punished by death.

She explained that the belief that reincarnation does not exist continues to this day, but when people realize that reincarnation is real, and they have the opportunity to heal any issue that occurred in any given lifetime, fear becomes less of a factor.

I understood. It was the idea of eternal retribution that had made me question a life of faith from the time I was young. The fire-and-brimstone, burn-in-hell sermons haunted me still. But I was now learning that the foundation they were based on wasn't even true. I breathed a sigh of relief, realizing that errors in judgment don't automatically mean we are going to a place called hell. Errors in judgment can be corrected and will be corrected as the lessons continue to be put in front of us until we get them right.

Susan went on to describe that through the process of reincarnation, we are given as many opportunities as we need to find our way. As light beings, we travel through the world of matter. We live many lifetimes in a variety of different eras, environments, cultures, and challenges. Reincarnation allows us to experience life through the ever-changing lens of our evolution. As souls, we eagerly embrace all the experiences the incarnations provide. Elizabeth Clare Prophet explains this concept in *Karma and Reincarnation: Transcending Your Past, Transforming Your Future*:

> Karma and reincarnation tell us that our soul, following the patterns of nature, journeys along a path of birth, maturation, death and then the renewed opportunity of rebirth. They tell us that we are a part of a moving stream of consciousness and that through many life experiences our soul is evolving. Karma and reincarnation explain that our soul, like the legendary phoenix, does indeed rise from the ashes of our former selves to be reborn and that our former lives contain the seeds of our new life. In other words, everything we are today we have been building for thousands of years.

"The perceptions that we hold when we die create our personality in the next incarnation, so we can work through any fears we still hold. We carry these memories in our DNA until we decide to let go. The issues we carry bleed through from past lives and into our current experience. Where we need to heal, souls and similar situations are brought back around," Susan said.

"I guess I can understand that. At times I feel as if I know a person even though I have never met them before. I have friends who've told me that they feel like other people they don't even know don't like them, and my friends can't figure out why. I am also terribly afraid of heights and can't explain it," I replied. "It's like something reflexes inside us that triggers a buried emotion."

"These are soul ties. They are the negative chords that bind us to the past. They are often karmic reactions to something that has happened before. The tie between a person or situation continues to loop through our existence until we release the negative emotion that binds us to the person or event," Susan said.

Susan explained that any person who appears to be the victim in this lifetime was often the perpetrator in one or many other lifetimes. On a soul level, when we have played a role in life, we often want to come back in and experience the other side; those who appear to be an antagonist in this life may have been the protagonist in another place and time. It helps us gain perspective.

Our guides give us experiences that help us truly understand others and hence ourselves. When we can stand in someone else's shoes, we can truly understand what it feels like to be that soul in that situation. When we see the world through their eyes, we can see where they are wounded and where they are blessed and what motivates them to act the way they do. As we walk in the shoes of experience, we learn the power of love and the power of forgiveness for each other and ourselves. We learn to offer the energy of peace and love to others. Any peace and understanding we provide to another shifts things, and an energetic chain of love is created that is stronger than brute force; the gifts of love and compassion open hearts.

The corners where darkness still exists will call for other opportunities and incarnations to heal and balance. So we come back in and try again. Behind the scenes, our guides are saying, "I have shown the situation to you this way, and you didn't understand. I tried it this way, and you didn't grasp it. We looped back around and set up another example for you here, and you missed it." But we have as many chances as we need to learn the lesson. The experiences show us not just in words then but in the vibration that is us.

"I have done past-life regressions, and though the scenes in them ranged from grass huts to royal courts, I recognized many people I know," I said. "One that stands out in my mind was a lifetime on the Great Plains. I was lying on a bed. I remember seeing red lines run through my heart and realized I must have been having a heart attack. My father stoically stood at my bedside. My husband in that life looked on behind him but wasn't allowed to do anything. The panic and fear I felt was intense as I asked them to get help. But my father insisted that, because of our religious beliefs, my death should not be interfered with. The soul that was my father in that life is a doctor healing people in this one.

"I also have a friend who told me about a past-life regression she had done. In her regression, she was a prostitute in order to make money to care for her sister and her sister's children. As she stood late one evening on a cobblestone street lit by kerosene lamps, she was stabbed. In her regression, she looked into the face of her murderer and realized that that person is her mother in this life. The person who took her life in that incarnation gave her life in this one."

Susan listened attentively, then replied, "Every person that we interact with in this life, we have interacted with at some point and time. Souls often want to come back and have experiences, and we have each played both perpetrator and victim in similar situations. We walk in different shoes so that we can understand the experience from the other side, because no one can truly understand a person's experience until they have experienced it themselves. When we do, we move forward with more compassion and understanding."

"It is humbling to understand that the perpetrator in a situation who we find so horrible could have been and often was us at another point in time," I said.

"The irony is that we are no different than a person we hold in contempt. If we are to release the cycle, we need to forgive the mistakes—our own and those around us. When we understand the truth—that what we give the world, we, in turn, receive—it is hard to do one without the other," she responded.

"Then that is why the Lord's Prayer says, 'Forgive us our trespasses as we forgive those who trespass against us,'" I said. "One day it will be us. Jesus was giving us a huge clue about how our world works and about our need to release the cycles that keep us anchored to emotional pain and suffering."

"That's right. Where we have made mistakes, we let go; we release pain and misery. We are able to see that we have lessons to learn and challenges to overcome, but we are not victims of them or judged for them by God. We forgive others knowing that we have walked in the same shoes. We offer peace to those blocked by the illusion; we offer compassion to those in need; we learn to love ourselves and in so doing, to love all God's children. Love, compassion, and forgiveness release any karma, and true healing is integrated across all our knowing and all our soul's experiences," Susan explained.

The Concept of Sin
Susan paused, letting me process the information.

"But what about what we have been taught? I keep going back and trying to understand the concept of sin," I said.

"Lots of people get caught up in the concept of sin and punishment. People often look at mistakes as sinful and forever noted in some heavenly file instead of seeing that situations occur to help us correct our path. Because of this view of sin, they hold fear instead of releasing it; they hang on to guilt and shame instead of letting go. But the reality is we are given as many opportunities as we need to see the truth. The laws of cause and effect continue to bring us situations that help us release the blocks in our hearts, but that has nothing to do with sin or punishment. Punishment is what we do to each other when we forget who we are," Susan explained.

"Sadly the concept of sin even makes us fear that God may not love us when we feel we fall short of doing our best. Religion is often where people turn to have a relationship with God, and it is often the very thing that takes people's power away. The problem has been perpetuated by the belief that we need a go-between to get to God. But we don't need anyone out there to make the connection. We just need to go in here," she said, pointing to her heart.

"Religion can make people feel unworthy of God's love and attention, and that is wrong. Why is it necessary to create fear in the hearts and minds of men? The idea that someone would burn in hell for his or her mistakes was born from the desire to control people. And fear goes against everything that God is about."

"I have felt this contradiction. It made me question everything," I said.

"The fact is that a judgmental mind is the antichrist, and original sin is fear. The concept of sin is just a tool the ego uses to keep us locked in the fear illusion. Its little voice will continue to tell us that we can't possibly be loved if we make mistakes. It will tell us that if we did something wrong, we can't possibly be worthy. If we listen, our wounds remain open and unhealed. Moving through life with a wounded heart, we interact with others who are also wounded. As wounded heart meets wounded heart, the ego weaves a tale that says, 'See, they would not treat you that way if you were loved and worthy,'" Susan said.

"But when we look at errors in judgment from a spiritual perspective, the meaning changes. It is no longer about the idea that we have erred, and it is forever noted. It instead becomes about God's love for us. We are reminded to release our fears and move into a life of love. Remember that Jesus did not have a lot to say about sin, but he did have a lot to say about love.

"Yes, we are responsible for every thought, word, and action we choose; we are inextricably linked to what we do to ourselves and others. It is the nature of the law of cause and effect. But when we are conscious of our actions and their effect on others, we make choices that reflect loving and positive intentions. We see our errors and know that we are given another opportunity to awaken and embrace our highest potential. When we see how important it is for everyone to see the truth, we approach each interaction differently. We make choices that don't negatively impact the vibration of others."

"I can see people taking that information and trying to be nice all the time, regardless of how other people treat them. I have done that too," I said.

"Being conscious of how we affect others doesn't mean we condone bad behavior—that doesn't help anyone. Allowing people to walk all over us is not being spiritual; in fact, that can create more karmic ties we just need to come back around and release later.

"And yes, our physical bodies feel pain. Bones break and muscles ache. But beyond the body, the light calls us to release the emotional ties that keep us looping through painful experiences that continue to pull us back in," Susan said.

"So we are not our past errors or faults. And wherever we are right now, God is pleased," I summarized.

"Absolutely! He knows the trials that we face, and his love transcends any mistake that we could possibly make. Once we understand that sort of unconditional love, it is easier to let go of all the darkness we have carried."

Reviewing this conversation later in my mind, I concluded that the true essence of Spirit, then, is shedding any and all blame and releasing others from fear and judgment. That release—the release of past hurts—happens through forgiveness and the act of letting them go completely. When we strip away what the ego would have us believe confirms our guilt, we find our innocence. It is an act of gratitude and love and not something that is held against us for eternity. It is the affirmation that we understand that we are all deeply connected to each other and working toward the same goals of self-love and freedom.

All the world's a stage,
And all the men and women merely players:
They have their exits and their entrances;
And one man in his time plays many parts.
~ William Shakespeare, As You Like It

Setting the Stage

Susan stood up and opened the sunroom window. A robin hopping along the ground took flight. A cool breeze rushed in, bringing with it the sounds and smells of spring. As she sat back down, she continued, "It helps if we shift our perspective and see that underneath it all we are all on the same side looking at the truth—all spiritual beings working on the same goals. Keep in mind that our bodies are vessels that house our spiritual self. They are the vehicles we use for spiritual education, and though it may not seem like it, in the end, there is no 'real' damage—that is just an illusion," she said.

"Hmm...it seems as if Shakespeare is right—all the world is a stage, and we are merely characters acting out roles that help us grow as souls. Then, life is a series of one-act plays and drawn-out sagas to help us see the unresolved issues that appear to separate us," I said.

"Think about it this way. When we see a play or a movie, we may get caught up in the characters portrayed. If someone does a great job playing the villain, it may evoke emotions within us, bringing the feelings to the surface for us to look at. The more convincing the actor is, the more we may experience a range of emotion from anger to sadness and fear. If we were to see the actor afterward, we wouldn't feel hatred toward him. He is merely an actor. Instead, we would congratulate him for playing the part so well.

"The same is true for us. We are, in essence, all spiritual beings acting out different characters and playing out scenes that show us the blocks in ourselves. Like actors on a stage, we rotate from balcony to front-row seat in each other's existence. Each interaction gives us an opportunity to share peace and love and learn nonjudgment and forgiveness," Susan explained.

"When we remember that all life situations happen for us and not to us, we can truly look at what life brings as a gift to reveal something about ourselves we need to see. Each person holds an aspect of that gift for us; each person is a mirror's reflection of what we believe. We draw people and life situations to us in order to share and grow and evolve as souls."

Susan and I both sat quietly for some time, listening to the chirping orchestra outside the window. Reflecting on what I had learned thus far, I started to see how important it is to remember that we all show up in life with our own knowledge, experience and perceptions. Every day we are challenged to understand each other, share our strengths, and appreciate our differences. The fact that souls are at different stages in their development and each stage of development has a different way of perceiving things can make relationships challenging. These differences are compounded by our various astrological signs, our past-life experiences, the influences of our environment, and our culture. But our interactions with others contribute to our understanding of life and ourselves—they enlighten us.

Every one of us comes here with a mission to achieve and lessons to learn. Since we don't know what anyone else's journey is about, it is not for us to judge the life lessons they have chosen or the blocks they are trying to release. We are all here to free the blocks in our hearts and move into a united consciousness, all interconnected and all in need of each other's love and support.

When we see that as actors on a stage we are all doing our part, we realize that situations are only good or bad when we see them that way. Yes, we may feel pain, and we don't want to underestimate what we feel, but we move through it and release the ties that bind us so we can stop reliving situations over and over again. We choose love over ego conditioning.

Showing up on stage, we move in and out of interactions, clearing the remaining debris. We reprogram our minds and see the dance for what it is. We move into a state of release, the contraction and expansion pulsing like the beat of our heart. Removing the walls between us, we move from defensiveness to receptiveness and from judgment to acceptance. We shift from constriction to release and from separation to oneness. We move through life in a state of grace, transforming from darkness to light.

We often look at the painful exchanges as trespasses against us and reasons to battle, but, in the grand scheme of things, they are really opportunities to see the wounds that need to be healed to release karma. The challenges are not difficulties we endure, but obstacles we overcome in order to loosen the ties that bind our hearts. There's not a soul interaction that doesn't help us with the process in one way or another. God has sent us each other to help us find our way. Any exchange with another, whether joyful or painful, is an opportunity to achieve self-empowerment and create harmonious unity.

But instead of sorting through and loosening ties, many people choose to battle each other. They raise their swords and act in verbal, emotional, physical, and mental combat. But challenges met with aggression create battles that wound hearts and guard hurt as if it were a prisoner of our minds. Hurts cause internal struggles that, in turn, create fear, anger, and a host of problems that lead to the breakdown of the body. They swirl around us, hide our grace, and dim the light we house.

When we have experiences that trigger negative emotional responses, the experiences are showing us wounds that need to be healed. We then have a choice to act negatively or positively. Where we find ourselves reaching for anger or judgment or even sadness, we realize that we have prepared for battle instead of reaching for the truth. And the truth is that the only reason people need to reach for weapons and battle armor is to shield their own wounds.

And people tend to pull others to their own energy level, even when they aren't comfortable there. As the saying goes, misery loves company. Even if we are aware of it, if we choose anger or frustration, we shut down the love/compassion energy; when we raise a sword, we lose our power to get out from underneath the issue. If we allow ourselves to get caught up in the drama, we sink to the other person's level, in turn, lowering our own vibration.

The outdoor orchestra once again filled my awareness and pulled me back to the conversation. "I have long thought that it would make life much easier if everyone we met came with a set of care instructions, like the labels in our clothes or the plants we buy from a greenhouse in the summer. Some plants just naturally need more sun, some need more water, and some do best if they sit in a corner without much of either. If people came with care labels, it might say,

'Wounded, be gentle,' 'Struggling because of the loss of a loved one, show kindness,' or 'Working to change who I am, please be encouraging.' We could follow their care instructions and feed and water them and monitor their ongoing needs. If we did, we would all coexist more peacefully," I replied.

"Jesus stated that more simply—love your brother. It may not appear so on the surface, but our actions and the actions of others always point in the direction of reclaiming our wholeness and holiness, no matter what the immediate experience or our interpretation of that experience may look like. Forgiveness is returning to the awareness and knowledge that we are all basically good and live together, working toward harmony and balance. The information we gain through life experiences makes the truth tangible. It shows us not just in words, but demonstrates the vibration. And when we hold it there, it becomes part of us," Susan explained.

"It all comes down to what we choose to hold in our hearts. Do we choose negative feelings like unworthiness, guilt, shame, or anger that create barriers that block the flow of life and diminish our self-esteem and authentic power? Or do we choose the path of peace, love, and harmonious unity? If we choose the latter, we open the door to profound and permanent healing, allowing renewal, rebirth, and unity of souls."

There was silence in the room. For a moment I could only hear the sound of a clock ticking. "That brings us to where you are right now, Mary. You have all the tools you need. Now it's time for you to go out and use them. If we were in school, this stage of your development would be called an internship," Susan said.

As I drove away that day, the farmhouse became a smaller and smaller image in my rearview mirror. I realized that I wasn't just leaving the farmhouse behind—I was starting Act III of my life. It was a new production in improvisational theater with fresh choreography and a feel-good script.

Entering stage right, I set a silent intention: As loving as he, so shall I try to be.

Dear Souls,
You have been invited to the stage of my life. May we stand in each other's shoes long enough to open our hearts in a greater way. Please take your places—the lesson will start shortly.

Lots of peace and love,
Mary

Moving from Defensiveness to Receptiveness
My mother had always been an organized person, but she was increasingly missing appointments, getting lost, and making mental errors, like forgetting to turn off the stove. She insisted she was fine, but it was clear that her Alzheimer's had progressed, and she needed help.

In family huddles, my brothers, my sister, and I decided we needed to find her a place in an assisted living facility that offered memory care. My oldest brother toured several facilities until he found one he felt was appropriate and, with an infinite amount of patience, he helped Mom see that this was the right thing and even a good thing for her. Gathering a few treasured belongings, my three brothers moved her in.

While my mom was adjusting to her new living situation, my siblings and I surveyed her condo and came up with a plan for the belongings that were left behind. Even though she had moved and downsized several times since my dad had passed away, there were still a lot of things to sort through. It felt odd going through the books and clothes and treasured mementos she had accumulated over the years. They demonstrated her talents and strengths. They were reminders of the people, places, and things she loved. But did they really define her? And if she felt they did, how would she fare without them in her new home?

The phrase "You can't take it with you" rang in my ears. It seems as if things we have in this life are only loaned to us for a while and then passed on to someone else. We don't arrive in heaven with a semi full of earthly belongings, backing up at the gates to unload them...*beep, beep, beep.*

So many of us spend our lives chasing material things and physical attributes that we feel raise us above the rest. We focus on what separates us from others instead of what brings us together. We climb to somewhere only to find it doesn't fill us anyway. I had been one of those people and was still identifying aspects I needed to shake. I was finding that sort of life to be fragile and conditional, shifting arbitrarily like quicksand under my feet.

Carl had often referred to it as "the sickness," and I believe he was right. Now that we were living together again, we had discussed the fact that it contributed to the demise of our marriage. We were on different ends of the spectrum on this one, though; neither one of us had had a healthy approach to "stuff." I had been the hunter-gatherer always on the lookout for the perfect something. He was like the squirrel, not wanting to spend a dime, ever preparing for a long winter, drought, or unpredictable storm. All that fuss over accumulation, and in the very end, we end up giving it away anyway.

Wrapping dishes and glassware, trinkets and vases in newspaper and carefully putting them in boxes, I wondered—what do we really *need*? Can we remain fluid and flowing in life if we are anchored to too much? Does focusing on possessions—whether it be material, power, or control—really serve us in the end or keep us from the goals we came here to achieve? What karma do we create when we set ourselves apart, amassing large sums of cash that sit idle in accounts just in case, while others live on the streets or traverse entire countries in search of a meal? Is accumulating stuff merely a distraction from the real work we are here to do, the relationships we are meant to strengthen, and the people we are meant to support, take care of, and uplift?

Little by little, the condo echoed emptiness, and our cars were filled with boxes of things to distribute among our families. As we arranged what was left of the furniture in the dining room in order to sell the condo, one of my brothers came up to me. He looked me in the eye and said, "You know, you told us this was happening. You were right all along, and we should have listened to you." Tears welled up in my eyes. I was so grateful for the affirmation.

Across town my mother was settling in. She had been reluctant to move and often told us that she would only consider staying in the assisted living facility temporarily. Still, this new living situation seemed to soften her. She seemed happier than I had remembered seeing her for quite some time. She was lighthearted and funny in a way I rarely remember seeing. Perhaps she no longer needed to be afraid of what she couldn't remember. And, I thought, on a soul level, perhaps she had the opportunity to release emotions that she was better off letting go of.

Susan hadn't been in her new apartment long before she realized there was a problem. Her nose was constantly stuffed up, and she was coughing a lot. This was odd, because Susan rarely got sick.

Then her cats' noses started to bleed. Realizing she hadn't just picked up a cold somewhere, she decided to figure out what was really going on. She walked around outside to investigate and found that the foundation of the apartment building was standing in three feet of water. In addition, there were water lines where the water had been much higher. Looking further, she realized the adorable, new apartment was in a building filled with mold.

Susan called the landlord. He said he would handle it. He never showed up. She called him back. He said he would bring tape and do a test. Again, he didn't show up. This went on over the course of a couple weeks, and by this time Susan wasn't feeling well at all.

She was upset and wanted to lash out at the landlord for being irresponsible when it was clear that this had been going on for some time and that he was affecting people's health with his choices. "I want to pull out my sword, Mary. I really want to," she told me when we touched base on the phone. "But what good would that do? His conscience won't even register what is going on. There is no sense letting someone like that pull me from my power. Instead, I decided that I just need to find another place to live. Once I find a different apartment, I'll call the health department to let them know that there is a problem so that other people don't end up in the same situation."

I was spending my free time writing and had fallen into a rhythm that filled me. I had awakened the creative Spirit within, and I was happily creating my heart's desire. I finally felt like I had arrived in a present I was supposed to be living. It was a powerful time as I watched my dreams manifesting.

For so many years, I had had that gnawing feeling deep within that I was not where I was supposed to be. During that period, I couldn't sit still. I ran from place to place. When I arrived, it still didn't feel right. I'd move on again only to find the same nagging feeling. I felt guilt for not being present, but I didn't know where I was supposed to be, so that in itself was absurd. In the end, it wasn't even about geography but feeling like I was on the right path.

I know I am not alone in this. Many people ignore the messages that call them to share a talent or gift. Like me, they often dismiss them as impractical or don't develop them, because they don't feel they can make a living using them. They push those messages into the wings in order to do what they think they are supposed to do, what they are expected to do, what the outside world tells us they should do.

Walking in those shoes, we often allow doubt to crawl inside us and fill that creative space with labels, like nonconformist, starving artist, or bohemian. We allow imposed expectations to cloud our thinking. We lose sight of why we are here in the first place and what we have to share with the world. We confuse fear with responsibility and courage with cowardice. Like a chameleon, we try to blend in with the crowd instead of standing out in our uniqueness.

Then one day we wake up in a life that isn't fulfilling and wonder how we got there. We realize we are running on a treadmill to nowhere and can't remember why. We recognize that we've attached our energy to other people's judgments. We feel unsettled, realizing we have bought into the messages—the labels, the insecurities, and the fears—that negate who we are, distract us from creating, and keep us from our God-given opportunity to shine.

And here I was, in the middle of my new beginning, trusting that the universe would bring what I needed. I was taking leaps of faith, knowing that I was being led to my heart's desires. I was learning what I was really capable of and discerning where the energy was taking me. I was filtering out the thoughts that in the past I'd allowed to sabotage my efforts. I was gathering up the shoes that represented old thinking and tossing them in the trash. The universe was sending me new shoes, and I was trying on a few new pairs to see which ones fit.

Standing strong in my resolve, I risked disapproval from my own ego and that of others so that I could find my own way. My ego's messages began to fade to background noise as the manuscript (and my life) took form. As in life, I was sure that each phase of the publishing process would hold its own fears, but I would face them when I got there. I kept the trash can close so that I could discard unwelcome judgments at any time.

I was finding that more and more people sought my guidance. I remember Susan telling me that you don't want to take the role of a teacher unless someone asks for it. Little by little, students showed up and offered the opportunity to test my understanding, read energy, and help them sort through life's situations without the need to call in action heroes or stunt doubles.

Without any prior warning, my friend Jane received business dissolution papers from her business partner's lawyers. Her business partner wanted to dissolve the partnership and start a business on her own. As one might expect, Jane, in turn, hired a lawyer to represent her business interests. But she and her partner still continued to work in the same office and tension began to rise with little to no communication between them. And once the lawyer's bills started to mount, Jane called me to ask advice on how to handle the situation.

"I look at this situation," she said, "and I ask myself, 'What does this person think went wrong?' Her lawyer said that she feels I am controlling. The tension in the office is obvious. Now everyone seems to be on edge. How do you see this unfolding?"

"That depends on you," I responded. "If you hold fear around it, it may not end very well. And you need to remember that it is truly a small world, and you may run into her again, since you will still be working in the same town in the same industry.

"I would call her. Explain that instead of trying to communicate through lawyers and spending ungodly amounts of money, you would like to work with her and come to a peaceful resolution," I said. "Face the situation. Don't be scared. And remember, you don't want to carry this around like baggage. You know that you will just be brought other situations that will show you that you need to handle them differently.

"Also, realize that what she is feeling is not about you. Don't allow her insecurities to become yours," I added.

A couple hours later, Jane called back to say that she had "faced the giant." She had faced her fear and called and talked to her business partner. They had decided to sit down and talk things through. The business relationship might not last, but the dissolution of it would be done with receptiveness and grace.

"It was such a relief. But my business partner told me that I am a micromanager, even though I hardly ever see her," she said.

"Well, is she right?" I responded.

"No. No, she's not," Jane said.

"Well, then you have a choice. You can hang on to it, feel bad, and act defensively, or you can see it for what it is—a judgment that doesn't reflect the truth. But understand that it is your choice. When we do choose to hang on to those feelings, all of the sudden we feel guilt, we feel shame, and our whole personality becomes off—even though it really doesn't reflect our authentic self! Instead, release it. Instead of projecting anger and frustration, send her peace and love. It will allow you to truly let it go. You can also put mirrors up to show her to herself. And ask for her angels and guides to help her see the reality in the situation. Then you have done what you could, and the cycle can end."

> *When you judge another, you do not define them,*
> *you define yourself.*
> *~ Dr. Wayne W. Dyer*

Moving from Judgment to Acceptance
Sitting across from Susan regularly, I had learned a lot about her. She hadn't chosen an easy path. Her calling was to serve as an intuitive healer and a counselor. Her life experience was a testimony to living in service of a greater cause. To a consumer-based society, her role may not have seemed very big. But in a spiritual sense, she played a very big role in the world.

I often saw her help people who were struggling with issues in such a profound way, that it was clear that they would never be able to repay her. It was a beautiful thing to witness. Of anyone I had ever met, she followed the example of Jesus, living simply, vibrating peace and love, and sharing her gifts freely with others.

At one point Susan was helping a friend who had heart issues. For the better part of a week, she focused on keeping her friend's energy stable, doing little else, including sleeping. I offered to reach out to friends and have them pray for the woman, but Susan asked me not to, explaining that she didn't want to add energy to the equation that might steer the situation in a different direction other than what she and her friend intended. Interesting—when we add other people's energy, we add to the equation. The end result is the collective intention, and we need to be careful whose energy we allow to contribute to what we want to create.

I shared the story with Carl. I hoped it would help him understand I needed him to contribute and not detract from what I was trying to accomplish with my book and correcting my financial situation. But Carl didn't understand—not the concept, Susan's gift, or why I sought her guidance. Instead he responded, "If she is so powerful, why doesn't she just bring herself a big house and lots of money?" It didn't help to tell him that she was creating all the time, not just for herself, but for the greater good and peace of all. Besides, she had totally unraveled that program and had little desire for material things. He still ran the program and judged her because she did not. I did what I could to explain.

When Susan and I talked, she wasn't bothered by the fact that Carl or anyone else thought these things. Instead she explained that it's OK for people to think whatever they want and that it's not our place to change their minds. She shared a story about a dream she had had in which there were hundreds of people at an event, all sitting together in one room. Someone asked a question, and everyone raised their hands to answer. In going around the room, it became clear that each had the right answer from their own perspective.

If we haven't stood in their shoes, we don't understand their perception. But from their perception, each is right, and it is a waste of time to change them. Instead, we realize that it is important for us to focus on ourselves, our faith, and raising our vibration. Where we see that we have something to share, we bring that energy around and offer it, but we allow others their views.

I walked in the house one day and heard my daughters in debate. When I asked what was going on, my older daughter explained that some kids from school were picking on her sister on a social media site.

I jumped online and read the messages. It had started as an innocent conversation about a posted picture. One backhanded comment had cascaded from slightly negative to blatantly mean as others chimed in. I felt like a momma bear, whose cub was being threatened, as I felt the sting of hurtful, judgmental comments that ranged from how my daughter dressed to who she chose to be friends with.

Even though my younger daughter, who was now ten, held her ground, it is hard to cope with repeated negative comments that are meant to attack who you are. It was bad enough when it happened in small groups, but I was finding social media took an otherwise controllable situation and fueled it into cyber-bullying. I had seen others fall victim to it, and I didn't want that for my child. I searched my quiver for pointed objects with which to retaliate. Countdown to launch...four, three, two...but then I came to my senses. Launch abort.

Once I had calmed down and the steam stopped coming from my ears, I copied the text into an email and sent the conversation to the mother of the girl who had posted the picture. She replied that the parents of the little girl who was creating much of the problem had recently gone through a nasty divorce. I responded that I felt kindness was a choice but that I could see how in her pain and insecurity, she may feel the need to lash out at someone. I asked that the mom have her daughter remove the conversation to prevent further damage and watched for signs of further issues.

I was proud to see how my daughter handled the situation. She had stood her ground and had not let these kids pull her down to their vibrational level. Instead, she demonstrated that she knew herself by not owning the negative messages being sent her way. I prayed that my daughter would continue to remain strong. I prayed that the other little girl would find peace and healing.

The magnetic life force brings people together, but once our hearts start playing a new tune and our energy rises or falls, we experience change. With that change, we may find ourselves in transition to a new stage with new actors and, at times, even new scenery. The shift from one to the other can be uncomfortable, but it is part of the growth process.

My daughters and I had been invited to my girlfriend's house for the day. I hadn't seen her since I started working with Susan, and my life had drastically changed. I was so excited to share all that had happened and find out what was new with her, her husband, and her children. But things didn't go that way. Other friends arrived, and the mood changed dramatically. I was not sure why, but from gifts snuck under the table to a different friend to quiet whispers behind my back, it was made abundantly clear that I was now considered outside her circle. This may be where she was at; however, this was not a movie script I was interested in appearing in—not in this role or any role.

In my next conversation with Susan, I shared what had happened. "My heart aches realizing that we just aren't in the same place anymore. It hurts knowing this soul and I have been through fire together lifetime after lifetime, and we are now in very different places. The love I have for her transcends earthly experience, and I don't want to lose her," I said.

"Remember that relationships are provided to help us learn and grow. Souls come in, and we feel a strong connection, but that doesn't mean it's supposed to be what it was before. Maybe there's one little thing we are supposed to fix, but then we are meant to move on," she said.

I knew Susan was right. I needed to let go...it was time for this friend to take a balcony seat where I was concerned.

Our world seems designed for relationships that last a lifetime, but from a spiritual perspective, that isn't always the case. Once we have learned a lesson, often souls fade from our lives. This was something I needed to get used to. Maybe it was because of social media and watching people's highlight reels while I was sorting through my behind-the-scenes in edit mode, but I longed for that connectedness.

But if I was honest with myself, that feeling of separateness stemmed from something deeper. There was something else that kept me from completely trusting myself and others, allowing shifts in relationships, while, at the same time, honoring who I was and feeling whole. It had showed up as a feeling of unworthiness, and this experience had brought it to the surface. I traced the energy lines back to where it began. My mind stopped short in high school.

I started out as a very happy teenager, comfortable in my own skin. Then things changed. My dad's heart issues resurfaced. He went through a quadruple bypass. He lost a lot of weight and was frail. When we thought he was finally on the mend, he wound up back in the hospital, first with an aneurysm then again with an infection. My heart ached—I so loved this soul. It was hard to watch him suffer. I felt powerless to do anything to help. I would have done anything to be able to take that pain and suffering from him.

The stress of it all took a toll on me. It was at that point that our family doctor had started me on antianxiety meds, and I entered a foggy existence, allowing life to carry me along. I often fell asleep in class and overall started to withdraw.

My sense of powerlessness was compounded one night after a house party. Everyone had been drinking, and as the group dispersed, I realized I didn't have a ride. Two boys offered to walk me home. But instead of making sure I arrived safely, they sexually assaulted me. I hadn't done anything wrong, and yet I was so ashamed. I didn't know who to tell, so I didn't say anything—not through words anyway. Instead, I tried to regain control of my life by controlling my body. I manipulated the numbers on the scale, purged food, starved myself, and exercised with what little energy I had left. That horrendous eating disorder haunted me for years, as I weighed and measured everything in life.

In the process, I had almost destroyed my body. In my downward spiral, I had hurt many people. Trying to wall off my emotional pain, I had missed so many opportunities to live a life of joy. The eating disorder itself had ended when I was in my twenties, but it seemed the emotional wound hadn't exited with it. Was it possible that after all this time, I still carried all this around with me? I couldn't help but wonder how much of my life was affected by these two major life events coinciding. The memories were still painful. My eyes welled up with tears when I thought about my dad and went cold when I thought about those two boys who walked away that night, probably having no idea how much they had affected me.

I knew I needed to let go of the pain and move on. What those two boys had done was wrong, but I had allowed the experience to own me. I thought about the two boys and stated my intention: "I release you. I let you go. I no longer hold bitterness in my heart around you or this situation. *Please* leave."

I had shifted my focus from my business to my book, and my business sat virtually untouched. I searched my heart to understand how much more I should be doing with the business at this point. I decided to attend a business seminar, feeling as if perhaps I would find the answers there.

During the meeting, I was asked to share a tip on how to achieve success. I had often been asked to speak in front of large groups because of the level of success I had achieved. But in my past insecurity, I would trip over my words and question if I had said the right thing. Though I loved teaching and training, I truly had had a love-hate relationship with the stage.

But I was no longer that scared little girl or vulnerable woman. I was capable of incredible things. I felt powerful in my understanding of the world. I felt excitement for the life in front of me. As I stood in front of the room, I felt Spirit fill me, and the words exited my mouth gracefully. "I have found that success is less about motivation than it is about inspiration. Find what fills you, and be inspired to use it to help those around you. Do this, and you can't help but succeed."

As the clapping faded, a colleague from the front row said, "That's right, Mary." It was the sort of thing that could have been said a million different ways. While I do believe she meant well, there was a condescending tone in her voice. I looked at her inquisitively. In my mind I was thinking, *You don't think I know…you don't know who I am.* Truth is, she *didn't* know who I was. She only saw the person she thought I was—the person who had stepped out of the race. She didn't sense the solid foundation that anchored me to something greater. Or did she?

I realized then that people resist change in others. How often do we have the opportunity to grow, put the vibration in place, and then succumb to the views of others and fall back in that old, familiar groove? How often do we have the opportunity to grow, yet feel the sense of loss as we step out of old energy and stop ourselves? But it doesn't serve us to let discomfort stop our growth. It is important we remember that we are already perfect. God created us that way. No, we may not always act perfectly, speak perfectly, or do everything perfectly, but those things are not who we *are*. As souls, we are perfect and do deserve abundance, love, and success.

I was successful. I was loved. It didn't matter what she or anyone else thought. And this one-act play had shown me just how much progress I had made.

It seemed as if my guides wanted me to be self-sufficient. More and more, the appointments I had set with Susan didn't materialize for one reason or another. This time it was a monstrous snowstorm in the middle of spring. This storm brought with it all the beauty and splendor of the holiday season. Huge white flakes floated to the earth, gathering on the ground and accumulating on tree branches throughout the night. The valley woke to find a beautiful, winter scene that created delays and cancelled events.

The roads were impassable, so Susan and I once again talked on the phone, and I shared the events of the past couple of weeks. Our conversation once again centered around judgment.

"Judgment is paramount in the ego's trinity perception; judgment perpetuates its existence. We are provided daily with opportunities to move our perspective and release people from our judgment. To the extent that we take advantage of these opportunities, we are freed. Our hearts open, and we move forward as souls. We demonstrate to them that they too are worthy of unconditional love, forgiveness, and no judgment," she responded.

"This one is tough," I said. "We are all so programmed to use each other as a template of who we are and what life should look like. Even though we know better, it happens. But I can see that this is where the ego's trinity perception thrives."

"Yes," she replied, "a judgmental mind really goes against everything that the Christ consciousness is about. And consider this—everything we think we manifest in our life, right? So if we focus on the weaknesses, faults, and shortcomings of others and ourselves, we draw to us lower-frequency vibration. If we criticize others in an attempt to disempower them, we create negative karma. If instead we choose to focus our attention on the strengths and virtues of others, we create a higher frequency current within, shining brighter and giving other people permission to do the same. Where we find others judging us, we stop the cycle by sending love and forgiveness."

"I can practice nonjudgment, and I have an easier time forgiving than I used to, but where I feel others judging me, I still have a hard time letting go," I said.

"It is easy to forgive those who do not wish us harm. But Jesus forgave those who held darkness, fear, and hatred in their hearts—you see it in the faces of the *Pietà*. Even those individuals are loved and welcomed home. They are children that deserve love and patience until their souls get the lesson. In fact, when we would think they are the least loveable, that is when they need love the most.

"Forgiveness is about seeing beyond the ego's hold and loving the soul underneath and ending the cycle of disagreement, attack, and helplessness. Instead of judging others for who they appear to be or for their errors in thinking, we perceive in them the steps they have not yet taken. Instead of judging them, we send love and peace and use rose-colored light to diffuse the situation. We pray that the right windows appear for the truth to be revealed to them. We pray that the right teachers be put in place to help them understand. We ask our Father to bless them. For when we are the least lovable, we are in need of the most love. Say out loud and hold in your heart, 'Bless them, Father, for they know not what they do.'

"Blessing people is the ancient tradition that surrounds those we bless with a circle of light to protect, heal, and strengthen them. Blessing ourselves or others channels divine energy and strengthens our connection to our higher self, in turn raising our vibration. Blessing allows us to attract more of what we want and less of what we don't. It awakens future wholeness and brightens our way. When we bless those who have hurt us, we temporarily suspend the cycle of pain and release life's suffering long enough to create a space in which love and compassion can enter their hearts and their minds.

"We can also say in our head or out loud when we feel that we are judging someone, 'I release you!' This helps us detach from the experience and get back to living our own life. We are here to work on our own life lessons and not on someone else's," she said.

Then she continued, "From a state of grace, we create love without conditions and let all judgment fall away. When we let go of fear and doubt, we can release people from judgment and shed any and all blame. Remember that it is not for us to judge the lessons of a soul or the choices that they make on their journey any more than it is for us to judge a tree by the number of leaves it has. That is the business of that soul. And if we get drawn into the drama, all God asks is that we free ourselves of the judgment that would bring us back into the ego's grip. Instead of reacting in woundedness, he asks that we allow our hearts to open and show the world our magnificence.

"As life unfolds, it becomes more and more obvious where the issues remain that bind us to the illusion. We humbly take ownership for our own errors in thinking. We stand in the shoes of experience, so we truly understand the wounds that others have endured. Through experience, we become more humble, compassionate, and caring humane beings. We look behind other peoples' eyes and see into their hearts. We start to grasp their circumstances and the life lessons they face. We have a greater understanding and appreciation for where others would find themselves, and we wish them well on their path," she explained.

Choiceless Awareness
Susan went on to explain how we develop choiceless awareness or a state of being in which we bear witness and choose nonjudgment. With choiceless awareness, we don't discourage other people in their growth but allow and encourage it. We understand the courage it takes for each soul to show up every day and try; we cannot underestimate the strength that that takes. In this state, we meet each person with an open heart, and we do not withhold love, because they don't fall into our agenda. We show compassion for others as they sort through their ego mind. We anchor in our truths and anchor in peace and greet each person with a sense of oneness and not of separation. We see in

our minds the steps they have not yet taken, and we wish them peace instead of difficulties.

"Don't overthink things," Susan further instructed me in that phone conversation on that beautiful, snowy day. "Let life flow from the heart. We don't know what the experience is supposed to be, and if we put too much emphasis on what it is supposed to mean, we miss it. We don't want to miss what we came together to share. And remember that others who do not understand the grip of the ego may not understand the error in their thinking. They may, in their woundedness, see the need to be right. They may see the need to relive what caused them pain, not realizing that they do this, because their heart is trying to release it. Love them anyway. Let go anyway."

"It's an ongoing task, emptying our hearts and minds and showing up with those in the front row of our lives, applying what we have learned about ourselves and others and seeing past the illusion," I said.

"But when we do," she replied, "we open a space for more spiritual information to be brought that helps us to see the situation from a higher perspective and to experience understanding, compassion, acceptance, and love. We then are healed, and absolute peace is anchored back in. We allow joy and love to grow within us. Deciding to stay open and be compassionate is humbling at times and enlightening always. Yet, untying the knot frees us to move forward and draws to us those who would choose to see life differently. Internally changed. Externally moved."

The best memory is that which forgets nothing but injuries.
Write kindness in marble and write injuries in the dust.
~ Persian Proverb

Moving from Constriction to Release

I saw an afghan in a magazine I wanted to make. I went to the local yarn store and described the design to the clerk and asked if she could help me choose a yarn.

The store clerk told me that she thought it would turn out "ugly," but if I really wanted to make it, she would try to help. She looked around at shelves of yarn and declared that they really didn't have a yarn that would duplicate the afghan I had described.

I persisted and was finally told that I could use three or four strands of yarn together to create the chunky stitch I wanted. I left with a bag of yarn, satisfied that I had what needed to make my afghan.

At home I pulled out all the skeins of yarn and started to knit. I didn't have a pattern to follow, so it was a matter of trial and error. How many stitches would create the width I wanted? Should I use three strands together or four?

I was determined to end with a finished product that I was proud of, so when the first and second times I could see that the width didn't match the picture in my head, I unraveled everything and started over. But since I had chosen to use several strands together, I ended up with a tangled mess where once there was a beautiful braided weave. Each cluster seemed to have a problem area where I had to patiently, gently tug until I found the strand that was the real issue. If I moved too quickly in frustration, I just created tighter knots. Knowing I had to be patient and take my time, I allowed the yarn to lead me into the chaos so that I could undo every knot, start over, and create something new, more reflective of the result I wanted.

Such it is with life and deciding to forget about any mess we have made, tracing our issues back, releasing the knots, and moving forward, ready to start anew.

The knots in the afghan weren't the only ones I was trying to loosen and free. But the ones that seemed most in need of untangling were the ones with Carl. At the time I didn't think of it as healing karma, but I was aware that the pain of some issues in our lives were so deeply rooted that it takes patience and understanding to find the answers and release them. Still, I felt it was worth the effort.

Carl and I were never together long before another opportunity to "examine our differences" would arise, breaking our inner solitude, like glass crashing to the floor. After another of our arguments, in which I felt myself stepping right back into my old character, I realized once again that I had a choice: to remember who I was or to brew an energy storm worthy of its own name. And, instead of meeting Susan to clean out old corners, I was at her doorstep with a brand-new personal rain cloud to release!

"When Carl or anyone lashes out at you, see the truth—their egos have taken control and are holding them hostage, masking their inner light. Don't think Carl is unique in this—everyone has baggage," she said.

"Baggage is one thing, but hidden explosives are something entirely different!" I responded. "I can understand that he is wounded, but the repeated lashing out is really hard to deflect. It's hard to have things continually thrown at me that are long over and that I personally had long ago let go of. Ugh!"

"Don't battle his ego or anyone else's. Egos each think they are right; they each think they have the right to be upset. Instead, look at what is really going on. Carl is lashing out in his woundedness and trying to release something that grips his heart. Remember the story of the lion that could not be controlled until someone realized there was a thorn in its paw and removed it. We are all the same. We simply need to find the real issue and release it. We remove our own, and we allow other people to find where theirs are and remove theirs when they are ready," Susan said.

"I have gotten much better at not being the first to raise my verbal and emotional sword, but with people who push our buttons, it is harder not to get pulled in," I explained.

"Remember that we are not only responsible for our own actions, but our *reactions*. Instead of raising your sword in defense, say to yourself, 'How can I help this person?' Emotional swords are equally dark, whether we start an argument or continue it. Don't let words cut you. Instead feel the energy and what it is based in. Instead of getting pulled in, send peace and love. It will help diffuse the situation instead of putting fuel on the fire. Look at the situation from your higher self. Stand in grace. Your need for power, control, or fear will fall away," she explained.

"Underneath the battle armor," she went on, "we are all the same and on the same side—all looking for what vibrates as truth. We are all beautiful, spiritual beings. And when we clear the clutter, we see that all offenses come not from a desire to wound but rather from woundedness and a need to heal and be healed. Remember to release. Don't carry it with you. Remember that no battle has a winner. Lay down your sword.

"Understand that in any battle, we know that both the perpetrator and the victim were, at some level, in on this together. Any argument, fight, or even violent act was, at a deep spiritual level, planned in advance. At the level of Spirit, it was decided between them that a karmic obligation needed to be balanced, and there was a lesson to be learned.

"Where your ex-husband is concerned, look at all the good that has come of this. Think about it this way: would you be writing this book if things had unfolded differently? No, you wouldn't have had the time to sit and reflect and compose. Nor would you be showing your daughters how to untangle and work through issues. This situation holds many blessings, Mary," Susan said.

Over time, the cycle did repeat itself, and I got better and better at seeing what was really going on. Still there were times...

A couple weeks later, it happened again. On a quest to raise my energy, I found myself sitting again across from Susan.

"How do we release karma, Mary?" Susan asked.

"We send love," I said.

"That's right," she said. "We release others in love. No matter if we perceive them as good or bad, we send love. Say it out loud, and hold it in your heart, 'I release you in peace and love.' It will diffuse the energy. Then don't get pulled back into patterns that allow other people to define who you are."

As I listened, I thought about what she was saying. I knew she was right. At times it did really hurt. I knew that I loved this man, but I was finally understanding who I was, and I wasn't willing to give that up; I couldn't continue to wear the cloak of his judgments (or anyone else's) as if they belonged to me. I couldn't let his or anyone else's energy drag mine down. I understood that took me out of my power and potential to create, grow, and become. I prayed he would realize something different too, but the karmic cycle could end for me, and that was a blessing he had given me by meeting me back on stage. I no longer was willing to live in a past that was over, especially when all the good memories seemed to have been forgotten.

"Forgiveness. We cannot underestimate its importance, can we?" I said.

"No, we can't. It is important to the evolution of our soul to release and let go. We may feel pain, and we understand that is true for others as well. But where we have held onto hurtful memories, we need to find forgiveness, pulling the hurts to the surface and releasing them. Once we have done this, we may still have the memories of things that happened, but we no longer recreate the emotional pain, the suffering, when these memories come up. We then move forward, making choices from the present and who we are in the moment. While the pain we felt in the past was real, it doesn't have to be what our present moment is about. That is a choice we make.

"When we let the past continue to loop through our lives, it anchors us to that experience, and we relive it over and over again," she said. "Instead we live in the now and focus on our own growth; we worry less about what someone else is doing in his or her life. We show up for the present moment ready to share, letting go of old modes of thinking, feeling, and behaving that chain us to our past. If we can stay present, shedding all hurts and clearing the air as things happen, there are fewer and fewer wounds to heal.

"When we move past the ego's emotional hold, we consciously begin to discern from our heart rather than judge from conditioned responses. We release the negative judgments about ourselves and others. We let go of all anxiety, unworthiness, despair, and the idea that we are unlovable. And in some situations, we release and let go of the very people we've spent years and even lifetimes trying to get away from and yet bound ourselves to, because we wouldn't let go of the situations that caused the resentment in the first place," Susan said.

"It seems that letting go, and the shift in perception that accompanies it, is the heart of all transformation," I said.

"Absolutely. In the act of release, our hearts move from contraction to expansion and our minds from constriction to release. When we release, we see what really is," Susan said.

As we unearth the perfect expression of the love that is within, we release the invisible ties to those who we feel have left us, betrayed us, disappointed us, or hurt us, and we are given opportunities to express ourselves in love. For without forgiving others and cutting the chords of resentment, we continue to be imprisoned in an unfinished masterpiece.

Ways to Release
There are many ways to release energy as it comes to the surface. The process can be like yanking a weed and pulling it clean. But the idea is to remove the emotion associated with an event completely, letting go of any suffering that ties us in knots that have anchored us to the past and held us hostage. Once removed, we are free in that area of our lives.

Releasing us from the ties that bind us to the illusion is what baptism is all about. In reality, water draws toxins from our auric body in the same way salt draws toxins from the physical body. Water's healing properties cleanse the light we house, lifting off the cloud of fear. It is why after an energy clearing, we drink a lot of water and shower or take a salt bath.

Not only do we release through deep breathing, meditation, and cleansing with water, we release through sharing in conversations, through laughter, and through tears. We release through yoga and exercise and through the conscious intent to pull up peace and move out any fear and darkness.

Using conscious intent to release is very powerful. Through words of forgiveness, we activate compassion and understanding. In that state of being, love and peace flow from our heart and throughout our body and out toward others. When we truly want to heal our relationship with another person, the intention alone can move everything out of the way. Say to yourself or out loud, "I release you and let you go." We release everything in life that holds us and blocks our hearts. The old must die so the new can be born.

Cutting Chords

We all have chords that connect us to other people. We don't need to concern ourselves with the ones based in love, but we can remove the negative chords to relationships that drain us by cutting them. These negative chords are based in fear—fear of abandonment, being alone, excessive anger or depression, codependency, abuse, unforgiveness, wanting revenge, or any kind of excessive neediness. The more we are aware of these chords, the more we can manage them.

Doreen Virtue explains negative etheric chords in her book, *Angel Medicine: How to Heal the Body and Mind with the Help of Angels*. Note that while I use the term *chord*, because my understanding is that they are harmonic and resonant in nature, Doreen uses the term *cord*.

> When we have fear-based attachments to a person or an object, we form spiritual leashes to keep the person or object from leaving or changing. These leashes look like surgical tubing, and they grow larger as a function of the length and intensity of the relationship. So, the largest cords are to parents, siblings, and other longtime, intense relationships.
>
> The cords are hollow tubes, and energy runs back and forth between the attached persons. These are fear-based cords, which are always unhealthy and based upon dysfunction. They have nothing to do with the love or the healthy part of the relationship. Cutting cords isn't abandoning or divorcing a person; it's releasing the unhealthy part of the relationship.
>
> Let's say that you have a cord attached to a friend or relative who's feeling depressed or needy. That person will begin draining energy from you, like siphoning fuel at a gas station. You'll feel tired without knowing why. No amount of caffeine, exercise, or sleep will be able to revive your energy if the source is etheric-cord draining.

On a personal level, that means keeping the chords to relationships that feed and nourish us and cutting the ones that drain us. People don't mean to draw off our energy, but it is a natural thing that happens when we step out of our own power, letting someone move us from our peace.

We can ask the angels and masters to help us manage our etheric chords. I turn to Archangel Michael for help with this, asking him to use his sword to cut any etheric chords that are not of love and light. We can then send unconditional love out to those that have been disconnected. We don't need to know who is cut, but simply trust our higher self and our angels.

Archangel Michael, I call upon you and ask that you please cut any chords that are draining my energy. Thank you.

The gift of pure love allows you to bless others and accept them without condition, granting them the freedom to make their own choices and live with them, and giving your Divine Self the freedom to do the same.
~ Neale Donald Walsch

Lifting Others Up in Love and Light

With a better understanding of how interconnected we are, I could see how much individual lives affect individual lives. Understanding our connectedness helped me realize how important it is to anchor peace and love in my own heart. I worked to be bulletproof in my thoughts and actions, and like a work of art housed in a museum, I worked more diligently to guard that creation within. I asked my guardians, guides, and angels to provide powerful protection around my energy field to maintain my state of grace and not be knocked about by the harsh and bitter striving I saw around me. When I forgot, it wouldn't take long before someone would pull me down. But now when new fog arrived, it was no longer the kind of fog that clung to the edges of life. The fog burned off quickly, revealing once again the beauty within. Still it seemed much more work to replenish my energy than it did just to share it.

"This is in your conscious control," Susan said. "Once we learn to maintain and stay in the higher vibration, we can learn to share the energy with people without shifting our own. Instead of letting people bring you down, you can share what is yours to give. When you share your energy with those who have a lower vibration, you raise them up. Like the light from a candle, we can help others shine without losing our own flame."

"We do this in the same way when we are projecting light out in front of us as we create our own path. First, make sure you are protected," Susan shared. "Then project light out from your heart with the intention that you want to share. In this way, you can feed someone else's flame without it dowsing your own.

"By sharing love and light, you can bring great comfort, hope, and healing to others. Put more rose-colored energy in your energy field to create a harmonious atmosphere and diffuse situations. Project joy, love, and forgiveness to a world that is hungry for it," she explained. "I often project peaceful, blue energy out to the world, so that when someone prays for or asks for peace, it will be there for them to receive."

I offer you peace. I offer you love. I offer you friendship.
I see your beauty. I hear your need. Feel your feelings.
My wisdom flows from the Highest Source. I salute that
Source in you. Let us work together for unity and love.
~ Mahatma Gandhi

Moving from Separateness to Unity

One would think that after all this time, my spiritual questions would dissipate, but instead I was more open to learning than ever. But Susan was very busy with her transition to a different apartment, and it was not a good time for me to pick her brain with a lot of whys and what ifs. And instead of turning to Archangel Michael, I looked at the wooden "Pietà" sitting now on my shelf and decided to talk to Jesus.

Even though I had been studying his philosophies and his life, I had not yet truly tapped into Jesus's energy to understand how he could be so loving and compassionate in the face of incomprehensible adversity. But when I did, I was washed with a beautiful sensation of peace and acceptance. In that moment, I had a much better understanding of what it meant to develop a life of individual Christhood and a life of faith. I felt incredible unconditional love.

I spent days testing this newfound connection. I would simply call his name, "Jesus?" and the energy would enter through my solar plexus, fill my body, and rest in my heart. I felt different, but all of a sudden people noticed the shift in my energy. People who passed by me every day without saying a word were now stopping me to introduce themselves and chat.

When I had a chance to talk to Susan, I explained what happened. "I thought you knew…that is the energy that I tap into," she said. "Jesus is the Master of all master teachers, and he tapped directly into the energy of God. Now you have a better understanding of what that love is about. It is hard to comprehend such a great love, isn't it? Now that you have found it, you will want to shout it from the rooftops, but remember that we need to let people come to it on their own when they are ready," she said.

"Our spiritual path is about creating oneness with all parts of God. Once we find peace within ourselves, we share it, creating harmonious unity in our relationships with others," Susan said. "We no longer see others as our enemies, but as spiritual beings all on the same path we are. We see past their ego selves and recognize the light within. When we no longer see other people as enemies, we allow them the room to take the steps they need to break free, just as we have. We overcome the separation that exists between us."

"In other words, in deep and profound example, we love our neighbors as ourselves, understanding that what we do unto them we do unto ourselves," I said.

"Every kindness, every act of selfless love brings us closer to our oneness. Every spiritual act ripples out and touches others in a way we cannot begin to fathom. Through acts of selfless love, we raise each other up and assist in helping others see the light. As we grow our light, we meet each other from a place of love and not of ego. Holding love in our hearts, we greet each other in harmony instead of opposition, in wholeness instead of fragmentation. We work together so that we not only survive but are transformed by the experience," she replied.

Ainslie McLeod describes this in his book *The Transformation, Healing Your Past Lives to Realize Your Soul's Potential*

> Without your fears acting like a ball and chain, holding you back from achieving your true potential, you'll have the confidence to manifest your goals, to be all you were meant to be.
>
> And what does it mean to be all you were meant to be? To put it simply, it means manifesting your true self—one that's both physical and spiritual. Your personal transformation will imbue you with a sense of purpose and meaning. And when that happens, you'll act as an inspiration to others. Your transformation will raise the consciousness of those around you. Without even having to try, you'll become a force for change. You will become the Transformation.

Every moment became a chance to breathe deeply of the experience. Every interaction with another became an opportunity for mutual blessing and mutual respect. Where once I might have been irritated by other people's choices, I was learning to find beauty in the vast colorful range of likes and dislikes and the portrait created when we hold them close together.

The question then became, could I continue to refine who I was in that state of grace and every day be a better version of myself? Could I help the world be a better place to live through the raw materials I had been given? How far had I stretched to see what I alone could do? If Jesus could sacrifice everything for us, could I offer my talents, my gifts, my life to reinforce his message?

My personal goals were no longer just about me and mine. I sat in silence and appreciation. Anchored in peace, I felt a presence knocking at the door of my heart. When I answered, I felt the energy of individual Christhood enter and bring with it greater understanding for the process and the goal. I had tapped into the energy of Jesus and, through Jesus, the power of love I had never experienced before.

With new eyes I looked at the world as an opportunity to be an agent of change. I saw my life's path as an opportunity to raise others up to all that they can be. My life had become about more than the earthly experience and balancing karma; it is now about remembering our oneness and, in the spirit of cooperation, raising others up through my example and through my talents and gifts and being of service.

When we share our gifts and help others through spiritual acts, we help those less fortunate than ourselves, knowing that we have walked in those shoes and longed for someone to raise us up. Around every corner there is an opportunity to be that energy for someone else and therefore ourselves. This book would be one such opportunity.

Listening to my heart, I realized there were other desires that lie within that longed to be expressed, and it was time to use what I had learned in order to create them. I prayed for guidance. I searched for the strength for what would come next.

And Lead Us Not into
Temptation,
But Deliver Us from Evil.

6

*Darkness cannot drive out darkness; only light can do that.
Hate cannot drive out hate; only love can do that.*
~ Dr. Martin Luther King Jr.

Living in Harmony

The summer sun sat high in the sky, centered in a peaceful sea of blue. Rays reached down and kissed my cheek through the car window as I drove through the countryside to Susan's.

A couple years had gone by since I had moved back in with Carl. The manuscript I had poured my heart into over the last couple years was now drafted and sat on the shelf in my office. It seemed to be at a standstill. Many people asked me when the book would be published, but there didn't seem to be energy to finish. I had questions about the story line. I had questions about how to publish the book. I asked God for answers, but they weren't forthcoming.

In the meantime, the contract position I had taken had led to a job as a writer. In the process, I met new people and heard many stories about how others also had been affected by the great recession. The fall had been personal to me, but I was beginning to see that I was not the only one who had bought into the program and had experienced the collapse.

My personal life also seemed at a standstill. There were moments between Carl and I that were so beautiful that I wondered why I had divorced him and pulled our family apart. Unfortunately the beautiful moments didn't last, and, before I knew it, they were overshadowed by darker, much heavier emotions. Friends told me that's what relationships were like, but I saw a tug-of-war between hearts and egos. Underneath it all, my heart longed for something more. Surely the beautiful life I saw myself living was out there somewhere. And even with all of our history together, if it wasn't with Carl, I needed to face that fact.

Lost in the road that stretched out in front of me, I thought about what held me back—held us back? What were the real reasons we weren't moving forward in any direction—was it fear? Was it control? Was it judgment? I could search my heart and find the answer to mine, whether I liked the answer or not. Getting to the heart of Carl's seemed harder to do.

Arriving at Susan's, I wondered why. Why are we still drawn in by the illusion that blocks the creative essence we *all* possess by the power of our birth? Why is it that even though the human heart aches to feel complete, we buy into the half-truths or total illusions that keep us from true peace? Instead of heart meeting heart, we find ourselves in a dance with anxiety and stress, in an on-again-off-again courtship with power, prestige, and material wealth, or in a long engagement with loneliness and depression. Those were not the sort of relationships I was personally looking for.

I climbed the steps to Susan's new apartment. As always, she met me at the door and welcomed me in. Her new home was smaller but was brimming with the same vibrant energy. We sat at the same familiar table looking out onto the second-storey sanctuary. A world of life met us at the balcony door. The surrounding trees formed a canopy that embraced the elevated porch. The perimeter was lined with beautiful flowerbeds and strawberry and tomato plants. There were squirrels and robins and an old, familiar crow. Out of the corner of my eye, I caught a glimpse of a bluebird.

My mind shifted from the beauty that surrounded us to the issue that faced me. "We can have the most beautiful moments and the most profound understanding, and yet the ego shows up and pulls us in a different direction. Why is it, Susan, that we still let the ego draw us back in?"

"Even once we find a higher vibration, it takes effort to stay there. It's important to remain conscious of everything we do, keeping ourselves up out of the negative, holding peaceful energy within and anchoring in the positives. It is the only way to change what is going on, not just for ourselves, but for this planet. Nothing else can save our world."

Lead us not into temptation means do not let us deceive ourselves into believing that we can relate in peace to God or to our brothers with ANYTHING external.
~ A Course in Miracles

Temptation

"It is hard at times not to look to the world outside ourselves for the keys to happiness. Any way you slice it—materially, mentally, or spiritually—there are things that masquerade as the answer. With any one of these things, we can find ourselves comparing who we are to someone else and think *they* are happy and that *they* have the answer," I said.

"I know from the outside it looks as if people who appear to have what we don't are happier and more fulfilled, but most often that is not the case. More often than not, they are looking for something to fill what is lacking within, thinking things, status, external power, or relationships will fill that space that only the divine can. But you now understand that it's not the world out there that is important—the world is nothing without what is inside. Most want what you have found, Mary—peace," Susan said.

The outer pull Susan was referring to we often call temptation. Temptation is the energy that draws us back into the ego's trinity perception even though we know the answer lies within. It is the magnetic force that repels us from what our soul instinctively knows it needs to advance. And when we go where temptation calls us, we are living from a false self.

The Garden of Eden
"This has been going on for a long time. The ego has been gaining control ever since the battle of Lucifer and Archangel Michael. It has been used as a tool of darkness in order to control and manipulate every thought, every perception and deep-rooted belief system. Where we let it continue to grip us, we remain imprisoned," Susan explained.

"Do you have a sense of what actually happened in the Garden of Eden?" I asked.

"My understanding of the Garden of Eden is that Adam and Eve were tempted by animal instincts. They saw the law of cause and the effect in nature, were curious, and wanted to participate. The forbidden fruit represents the consciousness of the ego's trinity perception—the mindset of separation, duality, and relative truth," she said.

"And as the story goes, partaking of it was a choice we made," I responded, confirming my understanding.

"We may have made the choice to experience cause and effect, but the ego was never meant to have this much power. Yes, we want the ego to help us meet our physical body's needs, but beyond that, it doesn't serve us, and right now it is out of control. That insidious control has us continually searching outside ourselves for what we know we can only find within. All because, instead of using the tools we were given to create a better foundation for everyone, we squander them on our own desires," she said.

As Gary Zukav says in the *Seat of the Soul*:

> The world as we know it has been built without the consciousness of soul. It has been built with the consciousness of the personality. Everything within our world reflects personality energy. We believe that what we can see and smell and touch and feel and taste is all there is to the world. We believe that we are not responsible for the consequences of our actions. We act as though we are not affected when we take and take and take. We strive for external power and in that striving we create a destructive competition.

Recognizing Temptation

"It's the idea of want, Mary. We have put so much importance on 'stuff.' We put too much emphasis on material things. They have become our idols and our whole focus to the point where we covet what our neighbor has. That is not what God would have us do. When we manifest homes, cars, or other material things, we see that's not what happiness is about anyway. It's just a whole different set of issues," Susan explained.

When I nodded in understanding, she continued, "If we are using material things, power, or prestige as weights and measures of our worth, we create malalignment; anytime we are thinking *mine, mine, mine*, we're listening to our egos. And allowing someone to control our perceptions or trying to control someone else's is a problem, and honestly, one is not a greater problem than the other.

"All darkness feeds off of fear, and the need to feel powerful outside ourselves may bring material wealth and worldly status, but at whose expense? We need to make sure that we are creating with the highest integrity where *everyone* is concerned. It cannot be done at someone else's expense. Until we see that we can only survive if we live from love and compassion, we are headed down the wrong path," she said.

"I know when I feel anchored in peace, life feels so complete. But it also seems as if the closer we get to a goal, the more the ego persists and the stronger temptation grows," I responded. "There are those moments when temptation is great, and the standoff between my higher self and my ego self is like a scene from the Wild West. My higher and ego selves meet in the center of town...it's silent except for the sound of the wind that whistles through the dusty corridor. Slowly, deliberately, my higher self reaches for peace. With fanfare à la Vanna White, my ego self reaches for a fabulous shoe collection, and the battle ensues. More often now, the shoe collection loses—whether because of the bunions they have created or because I understand the implication. But the battles still happen," I said as we both laughed.

"Shoe collections are the external world too, Mary," Susan said through her laughter. "Money is the external world. Money is a tool for us to use to create in this world, but money really doesn't buy us happiness! People consider money to be synonymous with power. Yes, money is energy, but it's man's creation, just like nuclear plants and microwaves. Anytime we are using something to keep something or someone down, that's wrong—that's not God.

"If we are using money or any other resource for something other than the highest good of everyone, we are missing the point. We are creating negative karma, and we will eventually need to come back around and clean up the mess," she went on.

"I understand that we cannot serve two masters, but how do we know that we are giving enough? How do we know that we are doing our part?" I asked.

"Yes, we need to take care of ourselves. This is not about taking a vow of poverty, but we are also meant to take care of each other. If we have the resources and know there is great need, how can we sit on our abundance and not feel moved to help? Right now everything is based in striving for more, and there will be no peace in that.

"Listen to your inner guidance. You will always be given the right answer if you ask and listen to your higher self. But that answer will never be based in *mine, mine, mine*. If that's what you hear, you are not listening to divine guidance. Share where you can. The survival of the planet depends on us sharing our gifts. What we are given is meant to be shared in order to create a greater capacity for light and love. This is not about personal gain. Personal gain is the ego's trinity perception and its illusion. Know that if you see suffering and do nothing about it, whether you realize it or not, it will haunt you on some level, and you will bring it to yourself," Susan said.

"None of the things outside ourselves can replace love; we have to stop thinking that money and other symbols of external power hold the answers. Money cannot help us repair what we need to fix."

Gary Zukav reminds us in *The Seat of the Soul*:

> Your evolution toward authentic power, therefore, affects not only you. As the frequency of your consciousness increases, as the quality of your consciousness reflects the clarity, humbleness, forgiveness and love of authentic power, it touches more and more

around you. As your temptations become greater, so does your ability to make responsible choices. As you shine brighter as your Light and power increase with each responsible choice, so does your world.

"I can see that mastering the power of intention and cocreation can help us with our personal and collective goals," I said, "but it is not, in and of itself, the answer and can actually open up new challenges if we succumb to temptation.

"The higher our vibration and the more information we have, the easier it is, at times, to come into this world and make a bigger mess. As cocreators, we allow the power of intention to work in our lives and create for the good of all and not just ourselves. When we move above the ego and work from our higher selves, as cocreators with Spirit, we become mindful and creative for the greater good of all. We must remember not to be selfish. We have a bigger mission here on Earth than accumulating things. As we continue to monitor our thoughts and see how they show up in our lives, we gain confidence in the process and understand just how much is possible."

We are a part of this world, but we should not be attached to it. Time and again we are shown to ourselves, so we remember what is real and what we should hold loosely to. We are shown what we have created as individuals, and we collectively are shown what we have created at community, city, country, and global levels. Our collective errors are shown to us, so they can be corrected and make harmonic union possible.

"We often look for our purpose on Earth as individual and separate from everyone and everything without realizing that collectively we have a much bigger goal to accomplish here. While people may say the Lord's Prayer regularly, like me, I don't think they necessarily understand that it's a call for peace—peace within, peace in relationships, and peace on Earth," I said.

"It may seem painful to let go of the things outside ourselves. But these things are temporary anyways, and letting go allows us to have peace not just in our hearts but across the globe. What good is it to hold onto material things and power if our world disappears? So what if wealthy, powerful people have a pile of things in a world that is falling apart? What good does that do them or anyone when we could have used the resources to help anchor in compassion and demonstrate love on a much greater scale?" Susan passionately said.

"There are those doing it already," she added. "You see more and more people opening up and contributing to the betterment of the whole, but we need many, many more to wake up and see the difference they can make. There is great need out there. We are at a critical time. The whole world is being shown what we are creating when we hold onto pain and misery. Tragedies are happening all around us, and our world is being destroyed."

"With all the terrorist acts, warring nations, shifts in the economic climate, and the strange weather we have been having, many are blaming God and predicting the world will end," I said.

"That's because people don't grasp that these events are a mirror's reflection of what is happening at the collective-consciousness level. Remember that we are part of a greater family beyond blood, nationality, and race—we are Archangel Michael's tribe. As such, we are interconnected, and what happens collectively in our consciousness affects the natural vibration of each other and radiates out into nature. Disease occurs when the environment inside the body is out of balance. Outside the body, an imbalance in the collective consciousness shows up as war, terrorism, and devastation in the social fabric," she replied.

Susan's explanation closely reflects the message Lynn McTaggart shares in her book, *The Bond*:

> But the crises we face on many fronts are symptomatic of a deeper problem, with more potential repercussions than those of any single cataclysmic event. They are simply a measure of the vast disparity between our definition of ourselves and our truest essence. For hundreds of years we have acted against nature ignoring our essential connectedness and defining ourselves as separate from our world. We've reached the point where we can no longer live according to this false view of who we really are. What's ending is the story we've

been told up until now about who we are and how we're supposed to live—and in this ending lies the path to a better future.

"Right now there is no place where there is no issue," Susan also told me. "We feel compression everywhere. The weather is unpredictable, and people are feeling it. The stability of everything is totally off. The more we hold worry and fear in our minds, the more we affect everything out there, and the downward spiral continues. It's time to realize something different. It's time we all found peace," she explained.

Susan was right. When I looked around, it was clear the world was in need. The United States still teetered from the mortgage crisis and the reckless lending that led to the collapse of the housing market. There had been a significant drop in the stock market that now rocked the world economy, and there were still people being laid off en masse as the economy struggled. There was the war in Afghanistan, the war in Iraq, and the terrorist groups that threatened more attacks on the free world. In the background, there was the pied piper's mesmerizing call to consume more, more, more and ads that offered the perfect, little pill to ease the emotional pain of it all.

Locally, there was political unrest in our state as Wisconsin held a recall of our governor. On social media and in gatherings with friends, arguments erupted as people took sides and battled to the end of their relationships. In schools there were random incidents of open gunfire. Online a proliferation of hacking brought down countless websites and drained people's bank accounts. Threaded through were grave messages about our environment and our struggle to sustain the earth.

In the workplace, I witnessed the duality as well. There was a sharp contrast between those who were truly focused on working together toward a common good and those who were focused on climbing, stepping on anyone who got in their way. I felt the tug-of-war that attempted to pull me from peace.

Collectively one day we wake up, look around, and wonder how the world got here. We gasp when we realize where we've arrived. It would be easy to think we were victims of it all and not responsible for the choices that created these issues. But as individuals we have defined ourselves, and we have collectively created the world we live in.

If we let our ego lead, we think fighting will bring peace. We may think money will fix it. Some just mask the pain and hide from the truth. Others appear to be above it all, accumulating more and more.

From an energetic perspective, none of these things are the answer. Creating fear won't fix it. Lowering the vibration through arguing and the need to be right won't deliver us from it. Putting ourselves on a pedestal above someone else only perpetuates the ego's trinity perception. With all of this, it would be easy for us to judge others who don't realize they were perpetuating the problem, but then we ourselves are coming from a low vibration. We all must learn to see people's need to heal as separate from who they are.

"Still we feed the very thing we do not want, and, in feeding the wrong program, we are totally missing the point. Instead we need to remember that people are meant to be loved, and things are meant to be used, not the other way around," Susan said.

"People pray to be delivered from evil, not realizing that the darkness—the evil—they want to escape is the fear they hold in their own hearts. I don't think very many people realize that the shades of gray they choose to live in have anything to do with the bigger picture. I have to say, I have been humbled when I realize just how much that has been me," I shared.

"As you have learned—for things to change, we have to change. For things to get better, we have to get better. And we cannot change our situation from the same level of consciousness it was created in. The problem is that in our separateness, we do not realize that everything we think and everything we do affects not just the people around us but, in fact, everyone and everything," Susan said.

"People don't understand the power we have through our individual thoughts and actions as energy beings to have a positive or negative effect on the world, ultimately the planet, the universe, and beyond. Every positive thought, action, and deed lifts us all up, and every negative thought, action, and deed lowers our overall vibration. Every time we choose to take or accumulate or focus on our separateness, we lower the vibration and overall frequency," Susan continued.

"But we can create peace if we learn to think differently. We don't need to be Buddha or Jesus to be able to change things. We do it by tuning in. We connect and commune with God and maintain an open heart; we work in harmony with God's universal energy. We become beacons that light the way for others. And when we go outside the walls of what the physical world says is possible, amazing things happen."

Susan stopped and looked at me, smiling peacefully. She seemed to be pulling our entire conversation together and listening to her own guidance at the same time. After a few moments, she continued, "Remember that awakened faith is about living our heart's path. No matter where anyone else is, we are supported by God on this journey. And as we take our next step, we can be sure that he will be there. We will be OK. Spend more time looking at the statue, Mary. There is more there for you to see."

When I arrived back home, I pulled the carpenter's "Pietà" from the living room shelf. I propped it up on the coffee table and sat on the couch to study it once again. Susan was right. It was clear that the statue did provide more clues. While in my examination, I had previously seen Jesus carrying a being representing us, I had missed the supporting structure that held both figures. The base of the statue supports the entire piece in the same way God carries all of us. He holds us all in the palm of his hand. He loves us all equally and unconditionally. When we feel alone on our journey, we can always count on God. We can have faith that God is always supporting us.

Since wars begin in the minds of men, it is in the minds of men that we have to erect the ramparts of peace.
~ UNESCO Charter

I was beginning to understand the responsibility we have to anchor peace into our own hearts. Where we do not, the vibration of darkness and external power says "divide and conquer" and instead of "unite in harmony and peace." On an emotional level, I could see how that pull affected the vibration of others, creating doubt, uncertainty, fear, and the duality of power and weakness. The energetic pull could be about politics, property, religious beliefs—anything, but in the downward spiral, negative emotion ensues and starts to loop through every experience in front of us. That loop then starts to spin, and as it spins, it affects others, and the effect widens, radiating out and affecting the energy of others we are connected to, whether they are closest to us in proximity or not. As usual, life's examples showed me the concept in a way that I could relate to it. When I returned to Susan's, I shared the story that helped me understand the effect we have on the world around us.

Normally level headed, my older daughter, now fourteen, was overwhelmed with the amount of schoolwork she needed to complete before the end of the school year. When her sister simply asked for help on the computer, she verbally jumped down her throat. They started to argue. It lowered the overall mood, and the negative energy they projected was like shrapnel that moved through them and out to me, then to their dad and through the entire house. It was hard not to get sucked into the vortex. The vibration had affected all of us, and we found ourselves in a battle that started with something small but had radiated out into something bigger.

Each of us went out into the world that day and interacted with many people. I would have liked to think that we didn't negatively affect anyone else, but I knew that wasn't the case. Energy supersedes, and chances are those who were not protected were affected whether we were in close proximity or not.

Weapons come in many sizes and shapes. Many of us are not proponents of war between peoples and nations, but we take arms every day to fight for something that tells our story our way. Even when we realize that emotional swords are as damaging to others as the ones with pointy ends and edges, vibrationally we feel the tug to stoop to someone else's energy level, and then we pick up the weapon in defense. These are exactly the little things that happen across the globe that create the stir that sparks arguments that start the battle that lead to war, moving us away from God's peace, love, and light. More importantly, how much of this exists in our world today?

"Not every battle is a war, but each is a tragedy. You will find that fear and judgment drive everyday decisions, create arguments, and tear apart relationships between people and cities and nations. How is it that raising our voices and raising our weapons in the end helps anyone? Meeting anyone with brute force will not bring peace or love to the situation," Susan said after I told her the story.

"I can clearly see that it doesn't matter who started it, either. If the overall vibration is lowered, and we chose to contribute instead of diffusing it, we too have to own the issue," I responded.

"Still the unity consciousness says that if any one of us sees the light in ourselves and follows that path of universal truth and enlightenment, that shift will affect each being around us. This happens in the same way you felt the shifts with your family. That gentle tap on the shoulder can and will bring us all closer to home, and we all have something to contribute," Susan said.

While it appears to the physical eye that I am here and you are over there, on the level of mind there is no place where you stop and I start. We are all affected by everyone else's thoughts, just as a butterfly flapping its wings near the South Pole affects the wind currents at the North Pole. When any wave moves, the entire ocean shifts.
~ Marianne Williamson

Collective Consciousness
Throughout my spiritual journey, I had been focused on seeing the notes that came together to create individual, energetic melodies. But I was now seeing the great orchestration as they came together and how universal energy is the unified life force that flows through

us, chord upon chord, melody on top of melody, with crescendos and diminuendos, blending and beautifully separating in its own natural rhythm.

When I looked at souls as variations on a theme, I better understood that we all exude light like a prism that reflects greater truth. The light demonstrates our strengths and weaknesses and our successes and struggles. If we could trace the line of color and intensity of this energy in detail, it would describe our soul's journey. The weave of all of us together creates an ever-changing tapestry of universal growth, perspective, and existence. In this universal symphony, each instrument is important and celebrated. Each contributes to the greater orchestration.

I was developing a greater understanding of how deeply connected we are and what it means to be cocreators of our own lives with Spirit. Beyond the unity of souls, I grasped, on a greater, level the interconnectedness of all things. Everything is linked at a very fundamental level by that same energy and universal force that echoes through oceans and plants, minerals, the earth's atmosphere, and mankind itself. We cannot be separate; we cannot be apart. Our separation is just an illusion.

There is a Buddhist Sutra, or teaching, that describes a net that stretches to infinity that is the heavenly abode of the god Indra. In each of the net's infinite vertices lies a jewel. If one looks closely, the jewel reflects all other jewels, which are each reflecting all the others. The net symbolizes our world and its inter-relatedness. It symbolizes a cosmos in which there are infinitely repeated interrelationships among all members. In the same way an arm is a part of the body and a leaf a part of the tree, we are a part of the energetic whole. The whole is reflected in each one of us, and the principles that apply to us individually also apply to the whole.

As a collective consciousness, our backdrop is colored by our collective thinking and our collective being. Every thought we create becomes a part of the collective energy force of the universe. It ripples through other people and the world around us, affecting everyone and everything—even the planet!

Anytime two or more like-minded individuals share a common perception, a united goal, cause, or intention, we collectively affect the unified pool. Like throwing stones across a calm lake and measuring the ripples—the bigger the stone, the bigger the ripple. The same holds true for universal energy—the stronger the vibration, the stronger the wave it creates.

In a clear sense of beingness, we can feel the ebbs and flows of energy that ripple throughout the collective consciousness. We feel the waves of sadness around the death of loved ones. We feel the energy that draws us in to shop around the holidays whether we have the cash or not. We feel the underlying negativity of war from the other side of the globe as if it were next door. Tapping into the collective consciousness, we feel the peace or sense the unrest.

"Look at what is going on our planet right now," Susan said. "The whole world is being made to look at what is really important. Everyone is screaming to the universe, 'What is going on?' They don't understand what is happening, but we are in labor, Mary. The unrest and instability are our call to spiritual awakening. Our world is shifting, but remember, the old consciousness has to die before a new one can be born. We have labored long enough. It is our time to master the balance between two worlds while maintaining an open heart and truly knowing who we are as spiritual beings—not just a chosen few, but all of us.

"Many blame God for what is going on around us, but instead we need to look to ourselves and what we are creating that vibrates so negatively out there. We know that light supersedes—then why is it so dark? Why is it so ugly? History shows the consequences of our choices. But what good is history if we keep repeating it?" she continued.

"It seems as if people feel they need tragedy and the law of polarity to be able to learn," I said.

"Why do we need strife to make a beautiful world? We don't need struggle—that is our ego talking. We need to ask ourselves, 'What voice do I choose to listen to?' If what we see unfolding is not what we want, we need to put a different picture in place. We need to own what we are creating. We need to understand the extent to which we own what is going on on this planet. We are not victims here—we created the world we live in," she explained.

"What is happening now is epic. We can't afford to let the aggression around us drag us down. We can't let the sadness of the world cloud our energy. We all must choose to breathe in peace, disengage from arguments, release judgment, and give freely of what we have. Each and every one of us affects the world, with the thoughts we think, the words we use, and the things we do contributing to the collective field of consciousness.

"Every hateful thought and word lowers the overall vibration, and every loving thought and word raises it. We can radiate out in darkness, or we can radiate out in light. When we radiate out in darkness, we create battles and struggle and misery. When we all radiate out in light, we shift the consciousness around us profoundly toward peace, love, and harmonious unity," Susan explained.

Our individualized energetic expression has contributed to the collective vibration. As a united energy, we are responsible for creating the world around us. The universe acts as a huge reflector, mirroring back to us the choices we have made and what we have given to it. From wars and terrorism to poverty and disease, we are not victims of our circumstances. Whether actively or passively, we each contributed to the world we live in and need to take ownership for the state of things.

We all play a significant role in the vibration of our planet. Our vibration also affects other realms and other dimensions beyond this one. The sum total of what we emit changes things much more significantly than we can imagine.

Living in a higher state of consciousness is a choice. We choose to see the steps we have not yet taken and know that peace is possible. If we don't have faith—if we collectively hold fear and doubt, we lower our chances of reaching our God-given task to create peace on Earth. When the world around us sends us messages that we should fear disease, poverty, or some unknown impending doom, we consciously choose not to buy into the lower vibrations. When we are invited to judge political positions and social issues, we move into a position of choiceless awareness. Where there is famine, oppression, brutality, and war, we send peace, love, and compassion.

Maintaining a relationship with God, we live love. Living our soul's path, we contribute to creating one loving, peaceful reality. How can we say we love God if we do not love the Spirit of him that we see in the world around us? Whether it is another person, an animal, a tree, or the earth, how can we say we grasp universal truth if we don't recognize the love and light threaded through creation and show reverence to all that is God?

You are not just a drop in the ocean.
You are the mighty ocean in a drop.
~ Rumi

The Christ Consciousness Grid
My expanded awareness had reached beyond humanity to mother earth herself and the field of energy that connects us all. Susan often talked about a planetary grid and how it would help us anchor in peace. I had mentally noted the information but didn't have a great understanding of its implication. But now I found reference after reference discussing the earth's electromagnetic grid Susan had mentioned to me. Often referred to as the Christ consciousness grid, this spiritual magnetic matrix is key to the birth of the new consciousness.

The Christ grid is fractal and holographic. It surrounds the planet and spans the multidimensional universe. It is anchored to the earth by its axis in Cairo, Egypt, and Moorea, a French Polynesian Island near Tahiti. Energy moves and flows along the grid through a lattice of lines called ley lines. Energy power spots or vortexes are created at the intersecting points of these lines along the lattice. The grid was known to many ancient cultures. They demarcated the ley lines with markers such as dolmens, menhirs, and mounds or earth works; they constructed monuments, religious sanctuaries, and places of worship to pinpoint and amplify the energy of the vortexes.

In an article published in *Atlantis Rising* magazine entitled "Earth: A Crystal Planet," Joseph Jochmans states:

In Ireland they are remembered as fairy paths, and in Germany as holy lines. The Greeks knew them as the Sacred Roads of Hermes, while the ancient Egyptians regarded them as the Pathways of Min.

The Chinese today still measure the Lung Mei or dragon currents which affect the balance of the land, as practiced through the ancient art of Feng-shui.

Much in the same fashion as the application of acupuncture needles in Chinese medicine helps the flow of Chi or life force in the human body, so the placement of pagodas, stones, trees, temples and houses in the environment was regarded as a way to heal the Earth.

The grid is an expression of energy and consciousness that follows proportions defined by principles of sacred geometry. Its lattice correlates to our consciousness in the same way the skeleton does in our body or a garden trellis guides vines, working as a framework enabling us to stretch, grow, and expand in a certain shape. In this way, the grid integrates emotions, information, love, and light, reflecting and amplifying the levels of consciousness as we ascend. We do not act in isolation but in concert with an immeasurable network of energy running through the planet.

Susan also shared that as we enter a new stage of consciousness, souls with a very high vibration, known as lightworkers, have been strategically placed across the grid to help raise the vibration of the planet. Anchoring peace along the lattice helps raise the vibration of our consciousness, and through osmosis everyone comes along.

While many cultures have discussed our connectedness, and science has speculated it for some time, we do live in an era where many feel the need to have scientific proof. Science has now proven we are linked to everything, and our connectedness plays a large role in how things unfold.

In 1961, Edward Lorenz, a meteorology professor at the Massachusetts Institute of Technology, was using computer simulations to try and predict weather patterns. The simulations led Lorenz to a powerful insight about the way nature works: small events (for example, a butterfly flapping its wings in South America) can have large consequences elsewhere (for example, can cause a tornado in Texas). This has become known as the butterfly effect. Lorenz's observations ultimately marked the beginning of a new field of study called chaos theory.

As Gregg Braden explains in his book, *The Divine Matrix:*

> Through technical phases such as "sensitive dependence on initial conditions" (or "the butterfly effect") and theories suggesting that what we do "here" has an effect on "there," we could vaguely observe the connection playing out in our lives. The new experiments, however, take us one step beyond.
>
> In addition to proving that we're linked to everything, research now demonstrates that the connection exists because of us. Our connectedness gives us the power to stack the deck in our favor when it comes to how things turn out. In everything from searching for romance and healing our loved ones to our deepest aspirations, we are an integral part of all that we experience each day.

What we choose to create has a huge impact beyond ourselves, and we can alter how things turn out.

Science now also theorizes that the heart is a powerful information-processing center that operates independently of the brain. In 1991, Dr. J. Andrew Armour introduced the concept of a functioning "heart brain" in a book he coedited with Dr. Jeffrey L. Ardell called *Neurocardiology.* Dr. Armour's pioneering work demonstrated that the heart has it's own functional "brain" that sends signals to the cranial brain and other organs. The signals, in turn, trigger the chemistry that is released in the body, affecting our emotions, perceptions, and our choices.

Science previously thought that the human brain was our decision maker; however, this new research shows that the heart is more powerful than imagined, functioning as a sensory organ, a hormone-producing gland, and an information-processing center.

In the HeartMath Institute's e-book, *The Science of the Heart,* Doc Childre, founder of the HeartMath Institute, a recognized global leader in stress management research, explains it this way:

We observed that the heart was acting as though it had a mind of its own and was profoundly influencing the way we perceive and respond to the world. In essence, it appeared that the heart was affecting intelligence and awareness.

These studies confirm what Susan had explained: when our hearts register negative information, we literally can't think clearly. Beyond that, when we are out of balance or blocked, we may experience the breakdown of the physical body through illness, emotional discord, and spiritual disharmony.

In contrast, positive emotions actually renew our physiology. They create increased harmony and coherence that result in dramatic, positive changes that include shifts in perception, increased creativity, reduced stress, and an enhanced immune system. Has science proven that we can heal ourselves through a positive, loving, harmonious approach to life?

In addition, science is studying our collective thought and, in fact, has confirmed that the world around us responds to and attunes to our field. We affect everything every moment with the energy we hold within and project out to the world. Holding a high vibration and radiating love can raise the consciousness of those who touch our energy field. Is science now confirming what Jesus said, *"What we think is given unto us"*?

Research was conducted at Princeton University for the Global Consciousness Project to detect the effects and interactions of global consciousness with physical systems. This project, which began in 1998, used a worldwide network of random number generators. The sole purpose of these generators is to generate a sequence of numbers or symbols that lack any specific pattern; random generators are the equivalent of tossing dice over and over again. The project found that in the presence of strong human emotions, the numbers formed an order that wasn't there before; something stopped the numbers from being random. HeartMath and the Global Coherence Initiative's report on these studies states:

Their findings have provided convincing evidence that human consciousness and emotionality create or interact with a global field, which affect the randomness of these electronic devices. The largest change in the random number generators occurred during the terrorists attacks on the World Trade Center on September 11, 2001. Even more intriguing was the fact that the random number generators were significantly affected some four to five hours prior to the attack, suggesting a worldwide collective intuition about the impending event.

This report refers to the very event that sparked my personal spiritual journey. Were the attacks on the World Trade Center the global alarm that awoke a sleeping consciousness of which I was a part? Had I experienced the collective emotion of a world traumatized by 9/11?

Currently there are random generators throughout the world that have been used to measure world events, including earthquakes and tsunamis. Researchers have found that overall the odds are one million to one that the generators would no longer behave randomly during these events.

Tom Shadyac's documentary, *I Am*, highlighted this research and suggests, "When mass mind becomes highly focused, something about the physical environment changes." In other words, it's not just the random number generators that change, but, in fact, everything we do individually truly affects what happens at a global level. Consciousness is the cause that affects the behavior out there in the world.

We are light beings who project energy through our intentions, and we are all interconnected. The field of our heart is part of the world and connected to that greater field and Christ consciousness grid. It is, in essence, connected to and interacts with everything throughout the entire cosmos. If we grasp this connection, then we can be open to the natural conclusions physics explains and the healing implications for everybody and everything. We can understand there are no chance occurrences; we can better understand the consequences of our choices, even the unseen, unheard thoughts—our state of consciousness.

Understanding we are heart centered is the first step toward effective change. Fine-tuning this instrument, we find peace within ourselves and with the world around us as a united whole. We transform every aspect of life until it resonates joy, beauty, and perfection—one peaceful, loving vibration.

Looking at the world around us, this sounds like a tremendous shift to make. But in order to create a shift toward healing, peace, and abundance, we don't even need the majority of the planet. Whenever two or three gather with a common intention, there is a stereo effect, an amplification of the vibration. Physics calls this phenomena entrainment, or the process in which two objects are entrained with each other.

Entrainment has been scientifically studied. While working on the design of the pendulum clock in 1656, Dutch scientist Christian Huygens found that if he placed two unsynchronized clocks side by side on a wall, they would slowly synchronize to each other. In fact, the synchronization was so precise, not even mechanical intervention could calibrate them more accurately.

Everything vibrates—everything from the simplest single-celled organisms to rocks to water to the earth to us. These objects resonate with each other. For example, if you play a violin and another one is in close proximity, the second will vibrate at the same frequency as the first. In this same way, as spiritual light beings, we resonate and match others' frequencies. We can raise each other up or bring each other down. (It is why protecting our own peaceful vibration is so important.) In this same way, we entrain with the environment around us, the earth itself, and the universe.

A scientific experiment conducted in 1952 on an island near Japan further demonstrates the unified consciousness and entrainment. In this experiment, scientists would drop sweet potatoes in the sand for Japanese macaque monkeys and then observe their behavior.

At first, the monkeys would eat the sweet potatoes, despite the fact that they were covered in sand. But one day, a young female monkey discovered that she could improve the taste of the potatoes by washing them in the ocean. She taught this trick to her mother and her friends.

They in turn taught others. The trend continued until ninety-nine monkeys had learned to wash the sweet potatoes before eating them.

Then something amazing happened. Once the hundredth monkey learned to wash the potatoes, suddenly all the monkeys on the island knew to wash them before eating them. Surprisingly, colonies of monkeys on other islands miles away also started following this new ritual without being taught.

In his book, *The Hundredth Monkey*, Ken Keyes Jr. explains:

> When a certain critical number achieves an awareness, this new awareness may be communicated from mind to mind. Although the exact number may vary, the Hundredth Monkey Phenomenon means that when only a limited number of people know of a new way, it may remain the consciousness property of these people. But there is a point at which if only one more person tunes-in to a new awareness, a field is strengthened so that this awareness is picked up by almost everyone!

Through entrainment, we expend less energy when we are in step with the surrounding energy. We find ourselves aligned and in sync—the same as with the Japanese macaque monkeys. When enough of us find peace within and express it out into the world, others will begin to experience peace as well without consciously doing anything else. And with lightworkers like Susan, strategically placed along the Christ consciousness grid, our goal to become aligned with the highest vibration in this realm comes into reach. Every heart that opens contributes to the greater goal. Together we entrain the heart of all humanity.

In *Awakening to the Zero Point*, Gregg Braden discusses this process and how it affects human beings. He explains the net effect of the earth's frequency on biological life and its vibratory influence as we attempt to match our base frequency with that of the earth. He states that:

> Each cell of your body is shifting patterns of energy to achieve harmonic resonance to the reference signals of our planet...This process is identical to that of the human energetic system (electrical

in nature), which may be considered a device of composite frequencies reflecting individual cell and organ complexes. This device, or module...our mind-spirit-body complex, when placed within the fields of another module (planetary or human) will have a tendency to move into resonance with the higher vibration.

In the human energetic system, however, the process takes on an additional component: the willingness of the conscious mind governing the body to adapt to the new range of vibration. The primary tool of adaptation is life itself, complete with the bundle of emotion, attitudes, perceptions, fears and beliefs that provide the framework for the challenges of life. One key factor in this process is the willingness of the individual to achieve balance within the energetic system using the tools of Choice and Free Will. These are the tools used to release old patterns of belief, lifestyle or relationships and adapt to a new more balanced pattern.

Braden reminds us that each cell in our bodies attempts to match the resonant pattern of the earth. He also states that the entrainment would happen more readily if it weren't for what we consider to be physical and emotional discomfort in the releasing, cleansing, and healing process of adapting to higher frequencies and consciousness.

Studies have confirmed that we can create a shift in the collective consciousness by amplifying positive energy and anchoring in peace. In 1988, the *Journal of Conflict Resolution* published findings on the International Peace Project conducted in the Middle East. In the study, a group of participants were trained to use transcendental meditation to create a sense of peace in their bodies, rather than simply thinking about or praying for peace. This group was positioned in war-torn areas of the Middle East in August and September of 1983. The dates and times the group practiced transcendental meditation were specific in order to control the effects of variables including holidays, temperatures, and weekends.

During the time of the study, they found a statistically significant effect and an improved quality of life that included reduced auto accidents and emergency visits, fewer fires, and less crime against people.

There was an increased stock market and national mood. The study also showed reduced incidents of war. There were fewer terrorist incidents, fewer war-related deaths, and a decrease in war intensity. When the participants stopped their practice, the statistics reversed.

Additionally, the study showed that with as little as the square root of 1 percent of the population, we can shift from darkness to light and have peace on Earth. Each person anchoring in peace can and will make a difference, not just to have peace in their own lives, but to save our world.

As carriers of God's light, it is up to us, through adversity and against all odds, to hold it bright within and shine it like a beacon through the fear and dark-ego storms generated by the world around us. We want to raise more than just the vibration of a few but of everyone. Since light begets light without losing the power of the original flame, we can feed those individuals with peace and love and light to help pull them up.

We carry the light of God out into the world as a torch—a reminder of the One who gave us life. Fanning the flame, we shine brighter and share freely to raise each other up out of the dark. Through a united, peaceful vibration, we heal the separation that brought us to this point.

Choosing Differently

In each of my sessions with Susan, there seemed to be a personal call to action and an accompanying story that brought the point home. My return to Susan's second-floor sanctuary on a midsummer's eve was no different. The blue bird I had glimpsed earlier in the season met me on the front lawn, hopping toward me and chirping, happily sharing a message I could not yet interpret.

The afternoon sun was starting to set as I climbed to the second-floor apartment. The steady buzz of nature faded as I sat down once again, and Susan began to share a story about a dream she had had.

"I was walking through the streets of a town, and all the houses were upside down. I was confused—there were no fires, and nothing had been blown up, and yet *everything* was upside down. Then my guides asked me, 'Now what do you do?' and I answered, 'Take what I have learned and recreate.'

"So ask yourself: 'What do I want to bring to this world?'" Susan said, looking into my eyes. Then she sat silently, waiting for me to respond.

"I want to share the knowledge I have gained in this process. I want to help make the shift to the new consciousness and higher vibration. That brings us full circle, doesn't it? Using all the tools I have gathered to this point and teaching others to do the same," I said realizing somewhere deep within that I remembered saying I would help. I remembered I agreed to move beyond myself and share a message to serve the greater good. I had found a teacher's teacher who reminded me of my calling and our true power and who had shared a statue and her knowledge to jog my memory when I had forgotten.

Together, as agents of change, we become one with the process of delivering ourselves from the grip of darkness or evil. We start with ourselves and work to hold a greater capacity of love and light within and project it out into the world. We keep the connection to God open and live from our higher selves. We anchor in peace and move forward with the understanding that what we put out there we get back and on a much bigger level than most would think. Prayer, meditation, and visualization help us create the new picture. Where we make mistakes, we pick ourselves back up, dust ourselves off, and continue to move together toward the light. Love, compassion, and forgiveness help us release the old consciousness and allow the new one to be born. We can then shift the energy and move back into our rightful place in the Holy Trinity as the sons and daughters of God, living in individual and collective Christhood.

We each have the power to change the world. We have the power to live in the light without the shadows of illusion. We have the choice to reinvent the way we live in a way that is sustainable. We have the choice to live our calling as miracle-minded, service-centered beings in the spirit of cooperation and not the spirit of competition.

Oneness is our goal, and it starts with the peace and love we each hold in our hearts. Through patience, kindness, generosity, acceptance, and forgiveness we create the shift. By amplifying the energy of love in us and around us, we have a monumental impact on humanity.

"Then creating heaven on earth is what humanity is here for. It is within our power to achieve this, but we can only do this in a state of goodness and grace, love and peace," I said.

"God's will is for us to create heaven on earth. Some are already there, finding beauty in the simple perfection of life. Finding abundance in things others miss. Looking past temptation, staring fear in the eyes, and reclaiming their inner, authentic soul force," she responded.

As we closed our conversation, I hugged Susan. I left in a new, more profound state of peace. Time to move forward and finish the book. Time for me to share what I had been creating.

It was also clear that it was time to move out of Carl's house. In the end, we were two people trying to support each other and on some levels—who knows how many levels—love each other, and yet we had a hard time meshing as a couple, because we had different ideas about what life was about.

I hadn't wanted to look at this scenario. The last time I had walked out the door, things hadn't gone so well. Working with Susan, I had learned that faith, not fear, was the answer, but until now not a mustard seed had been found on this one.

Even though the little voice in my head warned I needed fuel to fill my gas tank, food to feed my family, and a roof over our heads, and I couldn't possibly do it on my own, I knew that I could. Deep down I knew that little voice's message was just an illusion—I could make it work. In my heart, I had faith that God would help me find my path.

When I arrived home, Carl was sitting in the sunroom reading. Realizing that I was bothered by something he asked, "What's wrong?"

We'd gone back and forth on whether or not I should move out, but now I was going to make it happen. "I think it's time for me to move," I said.

Carl walked over and hugged me.

Emotion gathered in my throat. I was overwhelmed, thinking of the past, the future, the present. My eyes welled up until I could no longer see. "But I'm going to miss you."

"I'm going to miss you too," he replied.

We held each other for a moment. But as fast as it came, the moment was gone. Carl walked back to where he had been seated on the couch. While I was still focused on the emotion, he didn't want to stay there. He shifted the conversation and, with it, the energy. A different tomorrow would be waiting in the wings.

I wanted to process everything that had happened, so I decided to go for a walk and connect with nature. I set out on the walking trail that meandered through the woods behind the house. A light breeze swept by me. It was dramatically cooler than the stifling summer air I was wading through. The breeze carried a scent that foretold rain.

I reflected back on who I was before I had met Susan. I had listened to so many voices other than my own. I had shown up as a combination of messages that had absolutely nothing to do with who I really am. For years I lived under the impression that striving to become something out there was what life was all about. I thought that achieving success outside myself was supposed to make me happy, but it never did. In fact, it never was enough. It left me feeling empty and still searching for something or someone somewhere. Several times I almost shorted out because of it, sinking to such low depths that I thought I might never find my way back.

I had gone to see Susan with an ego agenda. I was looking for the "secret," but I came out with a mission. In the end, it was not about money or prestige or striving at all. It was about being true to my higher self and accomplishing what it was my soul came here to accomplish. It was about living in a way that love was the priority in every aspect of life.

I retraced my journey as I walked along. Nature's rhythm section was preparing for a musical set. The canopy of the trees above me began to rustle, and the ground foliage below me began to sway.

During my vision quest, I had often felt like someone had put me in a huge slingshot and pulled me way back only to shoot me forward. But because of it, I had seen a range of life and walked in many shoes so that I understood the perspective of many others. I had learned the power of forgiveness and now had a greater sense for who I really was.

I hadn't wanted what I was learning to have anything to do with love. I hadn't wanted to write about love. I hadn't wanted to acknowledge or open my heart to love, yet love is what it's *all* about. The journey to awakened faith is the journey to an awakened heart. I was beginning to understand the unconditional acceptance that lies at the core of the emotion and how sometimes the most loving thing we can do for ourselves and others is to let go.

The wind started to pick up, and the sky shifted from blue to gray. Still, I walked on.

The journey had taken me inward, descending in search of light and gathering all that masks its presence, clearing the shadows that clung to my psychic skin. Digging deep, I sorted and excavated until I reached the center and the eternal flame. Breathing it in and calling it forth, I listened.

It started with a whisper at my core, calling softly. Spiraling upward, it grew louder and closer, gathering an intensity that coaxed me to grow and change. It circled my heart, matching the beat and coaxing my heart to join its journey. Rumbling through my upper chest, it gathered force until it escaped my throat with great clarity. I gasped as I realized it is my own voice—my authentic voice—free from opinion, conjecture, and fear. It had a life of its own, a rhythm and confidence that integrated all my truths. As it exited my being, fresh and crisp and clear, it revealed who I Am.

The weather continued to shift. My voice joined with the rumbling in the sky, whistling through the trees. It circled and swayed with an intensity that grew beyond myself with an understanding beyond my own.

Claiming the ground under my feet, I tapped the rhythm that resonated from within. As it began to rain, I danced. I dug into the ground with my heels and threw my arms out to the world. Moving with it, I rejoined the web of life, blending with the rhythm rumbling through the earth as one.

For Thine Is the Kingdom,
And the Power, and the
Glory, Forever.
Amen.

7

One day, after mastering the winds, the waves, the tides and gravity, we shall harness for God the energies of love, and then, for a second time in the history of the world, man will have discovered fire.
~ Pierre Teilhard de Chardin

Creating Peace on Earth

The thirty-minute drive to Susan's turned into an hour. The dark sky that had hung in the background as I left the house had moved in. With it came a torrential downpour that blocked my view, making it virtually impossible to see the road a few feet in front of me. I pulled over to the side of the road and watched as sheets of rain came down sideways onto my windshield, pounding out their own story. I sat in my car and waited patiently as nature cleansed the land.

As fast as it had set in, the storm passed. The darkness receded as if nature was parting the curtains on a brand-new theater scene. The sky opened up, and the air smelled clean and fresh. The scouring storm had left a beautiful landscape that popped with colors and crisp lines that were more brilliant than any I could remember ever seeing. The world around me somehow looked different and yet the same.

My view felt clearer in the same way it did when I increased the prescription in my eyeglasses. The world itself not only looked but felt different now. I could feel the forces of change; the change itself was palpable.

Rain still dripped from the gutters as I climbed to Susan's apartment, and she greeted me at the door. As always, I showed up with questions.

"I don't really grasp how the ego became so powerful," I said. "How did we get so out of sync?"

"The times when the goddess energy flourished and creation energy was highly valued aren't talked about much anymore. If they are, they are talked about as if they are fairytales," Susan said. "Those were times of great peace, but somewhere about ten thousand years ago, things started to change. The ego took hold, and the world fell into a great darkness."

Ainslie MacLeod discusses the evolution of our species and how we find ourselves in a state of duality in his book *The Transformation, Healing Your Past Lives to Realize Your Soul's Potential*. MacLeod explains that fifty-five thousand years ago there was a dramatic shift in Archangel Michael's tribe, after which humanity was far happier and content. Wars were few and far between, and people worked together cooperatively and much more intuitively. MacLeod states that about ten thousand years ago, things started to change for the worse.

> As our tribes grew to fill whole cities, artificial hierarchies sprang up as we lost our connection to one another...Along with more formal religions and power structures came kings, priests, and other individuals who sought to take advantage of their position.
>
> After thousands of years spent acting according to our souls' core values, we became, to some extent or another, trapped behind what my spirit guides term the "Illusion," the invisible block between our physical selves and our souls.

"People forgot who they were. Trapped behind the illusion, the ego's dense fog, they felt separate from the universe, each other, and our Creator. They became focused on the world around them instead of the world within," Susan explained. "To awaken people once again to what is really important, Jesus was sent. He came in to teach every single one of us how powerful we really are and to choose to love others as ourselves. He demonstrated through his life how to live in an integrated consciousness. We are called to live in his example—that is what the shift to the Christ consciousness is all about."

For thousands of years, we have acted out of sync with our true nature. Behind the ego's illusion, we have seen ourselves as independent—separate from our world and blind to our connectedness to nature and the world around us, knowing our true purpose and understanding freedom lies beyond the ego's hold. But as we awaken, we see our reflection at a tribal level and feel the instinct to unite once again. This mirror reflects the need for a dynamic level of cooperation to transform our world. And working together we reach another aspect and level of our divine purpose—peace on Earth.

When we create from the Christ consciousness, we project peace, love, and light energy into a world hungry for compassion and acceptance. We overcome our fears and remove any blocks that keep us from making the shift.

When we choose differently, we give others the permission to choose differently also. The laws of cocreation are meant to maintain perfect harmony between individual cocreators and the whole. They are not meant for any individual to use his or her creative abilities to destroy other life forms or the whole.

"Remember, Mary, when we all live in the new consciousness, or absolute love, then the second coming of Christ has occurred. Imagine living in that state of peace all the time!" she said.

"And we are not too far from it now, though it may not seem that way out there. People all around us are accessing the light. People are awakening to this powerful, deepened spirituality. People's energies are being raised, and they don't know what is going on or how to ground themselves. That, in and of itself, can cause chaos, but peace on Earth is within our grasp. It is why the world is so overpopulated right now. Every soul wants to be here for the big moment!"

The world was a lot closer. When I stepped back and reviewed my progress, I could see that I was a lot closer too. My consciousness had grown, and I was on the edge of a big shift in my own life.

I had gotten past my block with the book. I was now putting the final touches on it—putting the wrapping paper and bow on my gift to the world. I had made decisions about where and how to publish, and people were showing up and offering to help. In other aspects of life, the future looked less clear, and I wasn't quite sure where the path met the horizon. I was watching for signs that would help me make a peaceful transition to the new next.

"It makes me wonder, as I often do about my own unfolding, how do we meet ourselves in a future that hasn't yet arrived?" I said.

"We dream it," Susan said. "We dream the most beautiful dream and go there often. And we ask, 'What if?' and allow it to be shown to us."

"As children, we are taught not to daydream, but we need to see our world the way we choose. If everyone saw our world in a positive and heavenly way fifteen minutes a day, we would bring it all into place. We need to visualize it, feel it, and make it real. And we fill the space in between with the divine power from within, shining brightly as the stars we all already are.

"We need to ask ourselves what we want our world to look like. This is not about jumping on a wheel and going as fast as we can and running and running until someone tells us it's time to stop. We need to get off the wheel. God said, *'In the stillness you will know me.'* He didn't say *in the rat race*. We need to pull each other out of fear, out of the darkness. We need to consciously dream a beautiful dream.

"Remember the dream of the houses upside down?" she asked. "When everything gets mixed up and turned around, we need to know that no matter what happens in the physical world, no one can take our inner peace unless we let them. In that inner peace, we are free regardless of the circumstances. And when we dream something different and hold that intention, we can move into it.

"But remember that cocreating and using intention are not just about what we hold within, but what we project into a world. So many need to be fed right now with light and understanding. It is up to us as lightworkers to demonstrate the walk we all need to walk to save this Earth. Every one of us who chooses this walk can affect not only our own lives but also our neighborhoods, cities, and regions and create a positive ripple across countries and oceans to areas where hatred and violence are so prevalent," she said.

"If I follow what you are saying, without temptation, then fear and the ego's trinity perception have no power and the illusion completely disappears?" I asked.

"That's right. Contrary to what people believe, the light does not need the darkness to exist. When we no longer see ourselves as separate but indeed one with each other and our world, the need for the ego's trinity perception loses its power. The competition we feel in our separateness vanishes. The need for power and control and weights and measures disappears. And when we no longer need to compete and no longer need to be first, we can rethink the way we see and do everything from our school systems to our political structures to our businesses," Susan continued.

"Anchored in our collective power, we see our responsibility and the effects of our choices. Understanding that every interaction with others affects not just ourselves but the collective consciousness, we are more diligent in our quest to stay anchored there. We move forward using love as the filter of our experience, living in 'thy will.' Creating in love and compassion instead of fear and the ego's trinity perception, we bring a new level of balanced harmonious oneness into reality—another step closer to heaven on Earth," she explained. *"For thine is the kingdom and the power and the glory—Thine!"*

"When we live the Lord's Prayer, and the prayer is our life, then after all this time, God's will for us and ours are once again, one and the same," I replied.

Never doubt that a small group of thoughtful, committed citizens can change the world; indeed, it's the only thing that ever does.
~ Margaret Mead

Then I ask—what if? What if we understood our connectedness? What if everyone saw the potential to join in this new paradigm? We could create stronger relationships with each other, our communities, our cities, our countries, the entire planet, and the cosmos. We could truly raise the consciousness of those around us and become the transformation that is needed now.

Dream with me a beautiful dream. Imagine a world where fear and competition no longer exist—our world, one community, where war and terrorism are removed and violence and crime are obsolete. Imagine a world where government officials are elected based on their compassion and openness to help each person and every living thing to the best of their ability. Imagine that schools, corporations, and economies are no longer about power and weakness or struggle and striving and instead focus on creating harmony, unity, and a higher vibration for everyone. Imagine each of us vibrating peace, sharing, caring, and working in cooperation.

What if we stopped looking to the past for our answers and the repetition of our history to understand what our world should look like? What if we tapped into the universal library, the Zero Point Field, for information and uncovered new ways of doing things, new resources to sustain our world, and new ways to implement them? What if we truly let the old consciousness and way of life die and collectively moved into something different that supported that shift? We would rise again, like the proverbial phoenix from the ashes of fear, hatred, and destruction. We would become the light we seek in a much greater and profound way.

Dannion Brinkley writes in *Secrets of the Light*:

> As we eliminate the need for darkness within ourselves, we neutralize its power in the world. Our personal renunciation of fear, doubt, and negativity in our thoughts, words, and actions will in turn cause the darkness in the world to diminish. Then we will watch as it gradually disappears from the face of the Earth...Then we shall take our rightful place as the bringers of the glorious and long-awaited Age of Peace on Earth.

"The new consciousness will bring us to a new level of awareness," Susan said. "It will reconnect us with our souls' core values, including cooperation, tolerance, peace, equality, and justice. It will give us a renewed sense of belonging and shared purpose and caring for others. It will be a time when all our physical needs are easily met—not just for a few, but everyone. It will be a time when we will all be free to explore our talents and experience our true nature as spiritual beings.

"We have already seen this level of consciousness demonstrated by many people, including Dr. Martin Luther King Jr. and Gandhi. They set out to create a better world without necessarily benefiting themselves," she continued.

"It is the message of John Lennon too," I said. "Since I started reflecting on the concept of harmonious unity, I have been seeing John Lennon everywhere—on billboards and pictures and hearing his music when I turn on the radio in my car. John Lennon, the Beatle, was a talented musician, but he was also a philanthropist and an instrument of change. He had a much greater understanding of the world than most grasp. When I listen to his song, "Give Peace a Chance," I wonder if people really understand that peace is possible or how much what they project into the world affects the state of our beingness," I said.

"While others struggle to find solutions through brute force, John Lennon, like all powerful men and women of peace, knew that the power of love far outweighs the power of darkness. Of course, the power of darkness will tell you that it can't be so—that is the ego doing its job well, but John Lennon had the right idea," she said. "What we really need to be creating is peace; it is crucial that each one of us takes responsibility as creator beings to reestablish peace on the planet. Instead of fighting brute force with brute force, we need to meet any action or reaction in love. We need to hold peace within and project it out into the world and diffuse the darkness."

"Remember the only real way to create peace is to be at peace and share it. It will have a ripple effect that will anchor in light. When we do this, healing will extend well beyond the health of individual recipients; it will light up the whole energy grid, the planet and beyond, with unimaginable benefits to the unseen world around us."

"Then each of us contributing can make a world of difference," I said.

"Each person anchoring in peace can and will make a difference. Pull up your peace. Breathe it until it fills your entire being. And walking through the open door, you can hold it open for the next awakening soul—like was done for you," Susan said smiling.

"Know that a vast network of information and energy is there to support us and to help us hold our vision and move into a new way of thinking. Having a strong foundation under ourselves is important. Going outside the normal walls of our understanding, we find our answers, knowing that behind every physical encounter there is a metaphysical meaning.

"We can let go of outcomes and celebrate being and the passage into something new. As we move past the duality in nature, we move into a new dimension of being. More metaphysical in nature, it allows us to continue our ascension beyond the physical body, vibrating higher and higher. And when as a spiritual, vibrational being we no longer fear death, we will, like many ancient cultures, transcend the life-death experience.

Coming full circle

I thought back to the questions I had been asking and the answers that came, each guiding me through the Lord's Prayer line for line. I realized the very first question I asked: "Is this what life is all about?" had been answered. I now knew without a shadow of a doubt that the answer was no. No, on so many levels, success outside ourselves was not at all what life was about.

I reflected on my vision quest and how I had focused and worked on each aspect of the Lord's Prayer until I had an understanding of the entire prayer. First, Susan helped me find God within and connect with Spirit. Then she guided me to have a greater understanding of the power of thought and choice and learn my soul's purpose. She had then helped me find forgiveness and release and let go of people and circumstances that held my heart in darkness. Coming full circle, I now had a much greater understanding of just how much everything we choose affects the world around us and is, therefore, sacred.

Did I have it all down? No, but I was working to perfect the basics and would continue to look at each aspect individually with a much bigger goal in mind. And none of it was about keeping score. It was about being authentic in a peacefully powerful way. Enough with the sadness—find joy. Enough with the competition and striving—find each other. Enough with the battles—find peace.

I was grateful for each lesson and the strength and humility to learn from them so that I could, from deep within, emerge a brighter and lighter soul, ready to help anchor peace and goodness and light into this world.

I compared my masterpiece in progress to the *Pietà*, the lovely work of art that had so often inspired me. With the *Pietà*, the transformation of a rough piece of marble into a beautiful sculpture is obvious. Unlike the masterpiece Michelangelo had created, the sculpture I had become didn't look all that different on the outside in the physical sense. Though the difference within me was obvious to me and many around me, there were many others who didn't notice the shift at all. But as with all of creation, new life sprouts first under the surface. Through diligence, patience, and tender, loving care, life takes root, sprouts, and grows into something unique and beautiful and visible.

Thus, the old Zen saying: "Before enlightenment, chop wood, carry water. After enlightenment, chop wood, carry water." The actions are the same, but the purpose and meaning are very different. Still it is humbling to stay open to possibility, knowing there is always more to learn. We never climb a mountain without another mountain peak on the horizon, but the discovery also makes it a glorious journey. The glimpse of joy, the feeling of gratitude, the roar of laughter, and the resonance of heart meeting heart brings us to a place where we better understand the oneness that ripples across multiverses—or multitude of universes into infinity.

As I reflected on my journey, the ebbs and flows, the trials and tribulations, and the relationships, including the one with my ex-husband, I asked Susan, "As I close a chapter in a book and a chapter in my life, I wonder, where do I go from here?"

"Our whole life is about learning and understanding and knowing our self and what life is all about. Every single thing you have experienced had to come into play, because it brought you to understand your greater purpose in a much bigger picture," Susan said. "Remember, everything happens for a reason. Your path has taken this course so that you can see your true worth, move into your calling, and be free to accomplish it. The universe has set it up. Go and shine! Shine, Mary, and show others what is possible."

"Time to dream a new dream," I said as I hugged Susan good-bye and walked out into the light of day. Walking along, I realized I hadn't reached the end. I had reached the beginning.

A gentle nudge within told me to look up. As I did, an eagle lighted from across the road. I watched him as he soared upward against a beautiful field of blue until he was hardly visible. I smiled, knowing that I too had taken flight. I was the phoenix that had risen from the ashes. My goal: the sky.

Appendices: Spiritual Tools

Appendix A: Meditation Exercises

Breathing in Peace

FIND A QUIET place to meditate. Sit with your feet planted and your back straight to prevent you from becoming sleepy. Close your eyes, and turn your focus to your breath.

Focus on our breath and work to tune out everything else. Breathe in deeply through your nose. Visualize peaceful, blue energy coming up through your feet. Pull it up through your body, past your heart chakra, and up through your crown chakra. Exhale through your mouth, and visualize the light pushing any dark or foggy energy through your crown chakra, almost as if there is a funnel on top of your head. Visualize, and like a bellows used to fan a flame, breathe.

As you breathe, use the mantra, "I'm breathing in peace and love and releasing stress and anxiety." Exhale and consciously let go of any stress or negativity. Feel the energy moving through your body, calming every cell and releasing the fog created by any stressful or negative emotions you may have been holding.

Meditation does not mean just sitting quietly for five or ten minutes. It requires conscious effort to be calm and quiet. If your mind begins to wander and you become distracted, gently bring your focus back to your breathing. It is also important to visualize the process. If you don't feel the energy moving through you, don't worry. Visualize and trust.

On our spiritual journey, meditation, like prayer, becomes a regular practice.

Cleansing Breaths

Another way to clear your energy is to use deeper cleansing breaths by drawing air in through the mouth deeply, filling your core, and holding it. Visualize the air reaching every corner of your being. Hold it as long as you can, and then slowly release it. As you breathe out, visualize yourself releasing any and all of the negativity you have pulled from your body. Like a tree or flower growing in nature, let it flow upward through your crown chakra. This will help calm the mental chatter and bring inner peace. Your channel will be more open to receiving information.

It is important to trust in our mind's ability to control our bodies. Meditation, like most things, only works if we believe that it will work. Our brain is an incredibly powerful tool, and meditation will help us tap into that power.

Appendix B: Prayers and Intentions

The following section includes prayers and intentions found in chapter 2. Use them to stay connected and to make your journey here as light as possible. When you experience challenges, they can bring you guidance and inspiration or the love and wisdom you need to tackle anything. Notice that most of them include language to ask for protection. And remember to always thank your angels, guardians, and guides for coming to your aid.

Angel Protection
Angels to my left, angels to my right. Angels above me, angels below me. Angels in front of me, angels behind me. Powerful angel protection surround me.

To the masters of love and light, teachers and healers whose intent it is to further the Christ consciousness on this plane, I ask that you surround me with God's powerful shield of white light energy and love—energy that protects me against darkness, fear, or negativity that may be around me or sent my way. Amen

Asking for Guidance
To my angels, guardians, and guides, thank you for your daily vigilance guarding my path and guiding my heart. I ask that you come to my aid,

providing positive information to my highest good. Any negative information that may be present, please leave in loving peace. Amen

Mirrors
To my angels, guardians, and guides, I ask that you surround me with mirrors to reflect negativity, darkness, and poor intentions back to their originator and completely away from me.

Using Light
I ask that the masters of love and light, teachers and healers, whose intent it is to further the Christ consciousness on this plane, to come and work with me now. I ask for powerful protection around my energy field. Please...
Follow it with an intention, for example,

- *Allow healing love and light energy to flow through me.*
- *Please fill me with the loving, blue light of peace.*
- *Please pave my path today with peaceful, blue energy and light.*
- *Please focus copper light where I need healing.*

Asking the Masters to Come Work with You
I ask the masters of love and light, teachers and healers whose intent it is to further the Christ consciousness on this plane to come and work with me.

I ask for healing love and light energy directly from Source to flow through me. I ask that I be able to tap into Divine Grace. Please open me to the energy of clarity and healing and help me hold the focus of absolute peace.

Appendix C: Working with Light

To work with spiritual light, remember first to ask for your guides, your angels, or the masters to come in and help you with your intention. Clear your space, set the intent, and then project light. Always remember to thank them for their help.

I ask that the masters of love and light, teachers and healers, whose intent it is to further the Christ consciousness on this plane, come and work with me now. I ask for powerful protection around my energy field. Please bring...

Follow it with an intention, for example,

- *White light, energy, and love that protects me.*
- *Rose-colored light that diffuses this disagreement.*
- *Yellow light that energizes my mind and lifts my spirit.*

Use the following table as a reference, but the more you work with color, the more examples you will come up with that will help you have a more graceful journey. If another color resonates with you, use it. The intention coupled with absolute faith is the important part.

Color	Intention	When and how to use it
Copper	Healing energy	Heals the body. Used for viruses, bacterial infections, arthritis, or anything where sending heat to the body may be beneficial.
Aquamarine	Peace	Anchors in peaceful energy. Learn to pull it up when you feel stress or anxiety. Put peaceful, blue light out in front of you as you go about your day and as your travel on the road of life—literally and figuratively. Ask for it to fill the room, your car, or any place you are spending time.
Rose	Diffuse negativity, discord, or frustration	Very helpful when dealing with other people. It diffuses anger, frustration, or woundedness. Creates a harmonious environment.
Yellow/Orange	Infuse joy and happiness	Infuses joy and helps move creative and intuitive energy. See yellow smiley faces on every cell of your body to pull up your mood.

| Violet | Purify | Purifies energy and raises the vibration in a situation. Whole books have been written on the violet flame and how it can be used. For in-depth information, read *Violet Flame to Heal the Body, Mind and Soul* by Elizabeth Clare Prophet. |

Glossary

Glossary

Aura or auric field	The human energy field.
Chakra	Each of the centers of spiritual power in the human body. Most schools of thought recognize seven major chakras, but there are also many minor chakras in the body as well.
Christ consciousness	A level of consciousness of the Holy Spirit.
Christ consciousness grid	The energetic field that encompasses the planet that unites the human consciousness.
Consciousness	The level of our awareness.
Dolmens	Megalithic tombs with a large flat stone that lies across two or more upright stones.
Earthworks	Prehistoric structures made of earth. There are three types: mounds, walls, and excavations.
Ego	The lens through which we understand our physical reality. The human personality.
Ego's trinity perception	The ego's cycle of power, weakness, and fear.

Enlightenment	The soul's ability to hold more light within and gain true understanding.
Heart chakra	The chakra is located in the middle of the chest next to the heart. It is the center where we give and receive love.
Higher self	The element of the human being that has access to God and Divine Mind. The essence of who we really are, the divine self that is living this life through us. We are actually spiritual beings playing at being human beings. The higher self is also referred to as our soul.
Holy trinity	Peace, love, and harmonious unity.
Integrated consciousness	When all aspects of self work in harmony and cooperation and our lives are not dominated by the ego.
Karma	The Sanskrit term used in Hindu and Buddhist philosophy to signify action followed by reaction. It is the universal law of harmony and balance that insures every cause set in motion will at some point in the future bring about its corresponding effect.
Kundalini energy	Kundalini is the light of the divine and sacred fire found in the root chakra, located at the base of the spine. When it rises from the base to the crown chakra, it quickens and awakens each chakra along the way.
Law of polarity	The universal law that states that things are the same just on opposite sides of the spectrum.

Lightworkers	Those who carry the light of Christ.
Menhirs	Large upright standing stones erected in Neolithic Europe.
Meridians	The internal energy pathways throughout the physical body that energetically connect a person's organs and their many subsystems.
Metaphysical	Transcending physical matter or the laws of nature, metaphysical refers to the forces in the universe that are not seen.
Multiverses	Multiple universes.
Piscean Age	The 2,150-year cycle that is considered the Age of Universal Peace.
Reiki	A healing technique in which an energy worker channels energy in order to activate natural healing processes and restore an individuals physical and emotional well being.
Reincarnation	The rebirth of a soul in a new body.
Solar plexus	The area of the body near the base of the sternum.
Zero Point Field	The infinite energy supply of our God or Divine Mind that is contained within all things.

Bibliography

Referenced books:

Braden, Gregg. *Secrets of the Lost Mode of Prayer*. Hay House Publishing, 2006.

Braden, Gregg. *Awakening to Zero Point: The Collective Initiation*. Bellevue, WA: Radio Bookstore Press, 1993.

Braden, Gregg. *The Divine Matrix*. Hay House Publishing, 2007.

Braden, Gregg. *The Spontaneous Belief of Healing*. Hay House Publishing, 2008.

Brinkley, Dannion, and Kathryn Brinkley. *Secrets of the Light*. New York: HarperCollins, 2008.

Bougnon, Lou. *We Are Here to Learn*. Johannesburg, South Africa, 2004.

Browne, Mary T. *The Power of Karma: How to Understand Your Past and Shape Your Future*. New York: HarperCollins, 2003.

Carroll, Lee & Kyron, Coiri, Patricia & The Sirian High Council, Lewis, Pepper & Gaia. *Transition Now: Redefining Duality, 2012 and Beyond*. San Francisco, CA: Heaven and Earth Publications, Inc., 2010.

Childre, Doc. *The Science of the Heart*. Boulder Creek, CA: HeartMath Research Center, 2001.

Dale, Ralph Alan. *Tao Te Ching: A New Translation & Commentary*. New York: Barnes & Noble Books, 2005.

de Becker, Gavin. *The Gift of Fear: Survival Signals that Protect Us from Violence*. Boston, MA: Little Brown and Company, 1997.

Ferrini, Paul. *Love without Conditions: Reflections of the Christ Mind*. Greenfield, MA; Heartways Press, 1994.

Guarneri, Mimi, M.D., F.A.C.C. *The Heart Speaks: A Cardiologist Reveals the Secret Language of Healing*. New York: Touchstone, 2006.

Hupka, Robert. *Michelangelo: Pietà*. New York: Crown Publishing Group, 1996.

Katie, Byron. *Loving What Is*. New York: Three Rivers Press, 2002.

Kemp, Andrew J. *Quantum K*. www.quantumk.co.uk/quantumk.

Keyes Jr., Ken. *The Hundredth Monkey*. Amherst, New York: Prometheus Books, 1991.

King, Godfre Ray. *Unveiled Mysteries*. Chicago: Saint Germain Press, 1934.

Lake, Gina. *Sojourn: The Soul's Evolution on Earth*. Endless Satsang Foundation, www.radicalhappiness.com, 1997.

Long, James A. *Expanding Horizons*. Theosophical University Press, July 1995.

Needleman, Jacob. *Lost Christianity*. New York: Penguin Group, 1980.

Markova, Dawna. *No Enemies Within*. Emeryville, CA: Conari Press, 1994.

Merton, Thomas. *Conjectures of a Guilty Bystander*. New York: Crown Publishing Group, a division of Random House LLC, 1965.

McLeod, Ainslie. *The Instruction: Living the Life Your Soul Intended*. Boulder, CO: Sounds True Inc., 2007.

McLeod, Ainslie. *The Transformation: Healing Your Past Lives to Realize Your Soul's Potential*. Boulder, CO: Sounds True Inc., 2010.

McTaggart, Lynne. *The Field: The Quest for the Secret Force of the Universe*. Great Britain: Harpers Collins Publishers, 2008.

Millman, Dan. *Way of the Peaceful Warrior—A Book that Changes Lives*. California: H. J. Kramer in conjunction with New World Library, 2000.

Moss, Andrew. *From Illusion to Reality*. West Palm Beach, FL: Infinity Publishing, 2001.

Orme-Johnson, Alexander, et al., *Journal of Conflict Resolution*, 32(4), 776–812, 1988.

Orme-Johnson, Alexander, & Davies, *Journal of Conflict Resolution*, 34(4), 756–768, 1990.

Prophet, Elizabeth Clare, and Erin L. Prophet. *Reincarnation: The Missing Link in Christianity*. Corwin Springs, MT: Summit University Press, 1997.

Prophet, Elizabeth Clare, and Patricia Spadaro. *Karma and Reincarnation: Transcending Your Past, Transforming Your Future*. Corwin Springs, MT: Summit University Press, 2004.

Prophet, Elizabeth Clare, and Patricia Spadaro. *Your Seven Energy Centers: A Holistic Approach to Physical, Emotional and Spiritual Vitality*. Corwin Springs, MT: Summit University Press, 2000.

Prophet, Elizabeth Clare. *Violet Flame to Heal Mind, Body and Soul*. Corwin Springs, MT: Summit University Press, 1997.

Redfield, James. *The Celestine Prophecy: an Adventure*. New York: Warner Books, 1993.

Virtue, Doreen. *Angel Medicine: How to Heal the Body and Mind with the Help of Angels*. United States: Hay House Publishing, 2004.

Waters, Owen. *The Shift: The Revolution in Human Consciousness*. Delaware: Infinite Being Publishing, 2006.

Williamson, Marianne. *Return to Love: Reflections on the Principles of a Course in Miracles*. New York: HarperCollins Publishers, 1992.

Zukav, Gary. *Seat of the Soul*. New York: Fireside, Simon & Schuster, 1989.

A Course in Miracles. Mill Valley, CA: Foundation for Inner Peace, 2007.

Journals:

Orme-Johnson, D. W., Alexander, C. N., Davies, J. L., Chandler, H. M., & Larimore, W. E. (1988). International peace project in the Middle East: The effect of the Maharishi Technology of the Unified Field. Journal of Conflict Resolution, 32(4), 776–812.

Websites:

"Aka Cords." http://kundalini-teacher.com/karma/akacords.php.

"Amplifying Love and the Rediscovery of Fire." http://kimcocreation.blogspot.com/2008/01/amplifying-love-and-rediscovery-of-fire.html.

"Ascended Masters Realm." http://lightgrid.ning.com/group/ascended masterrealm?groupUrl=ascendedmasterrealm&id=4024228%3AGroup%3A39994&page=3.

"Channeled Insights on the Nature of Intention." http://www.askalana.com/blog/channeling-nature-of-intention/.

Christ Consciousness. http://finalbookofdaniel.com/christ_consciousness.html.

Christianity and Reincarnation. http://www.topix.com/forum/religion/sikh/T5P07F71HU7VSR4SI.

"Creative Visualization Techniques." http://www.wingsforthespirit.com/creative-visualization.htm.

"Forgive Enemies." http://www.theego.org/christ-mind.html.

Hamrick, Julia Rogers. "Ego or Higher Self: Who's Behind Your Decisions?" http://www.juliarogershamrick.com/articles.html?article=ego&title=Ego+or+Higher+Self:+Who's+Behind+Your+Decisions?.

"Harnessing Power in the Power of Intention." http://practicalintention.com/?p=31.

Holt, Ronald L. "The Christ Grid." http://lightgrid.ning.com/group/gridinformationwhatisthelightgrid/forum/topics/the-christ-grid-by-ronald-l-holt.

"Influence of Neoplatonism on Michelangelo's Art." http://www.bookrags.com/essay-2005/1/20/2045/53398/.

"I Pray, I Meditate." http://www.srichinmoy.org/spirituality/concentration_meditation_contemplation/meditation/prayer_and_meditation.

Jochmans, Joseph. "Earth: A Crystal Planet." www.atlantisrisingmagazine.com.

Kearns, Kell. "The Consciousness of the Christ: Reclaiming Jesus for a New Humanity." www.heavenearth.net/tcotc_essay.html.

Long, James A. "Karma: Law of Cause and Effect." http://www.theosophy-nw.org/theosnw/karma/ka-jal.htm.

Love as Energy. www.teilharddech`1ardin.org.

Meltz, Lucille Ann. "Your Spiritual Mirror." http://www.selfgrowth.com/articles/Your_Spiritual_Mirror.html.

"Michelangelo and the *Pietà*." http://newrenart.com/michelangelo-and-the-pieta.

"Not Enough vs. Trusting in Abundance: The Warriors within Our Minds." http://www.powerfull-living.biz/blog/2010/10/16/not-enough-vs-trusting-in-abundance-the-warriors-within-our-minds/.

Roman, Sanaya, and Duane Packer. "Blending with Your Soul." https://www.orindaben.com/pages/newsletters/bldsoul.

The Ascended Masters. http://www.ascendedmastersoflight.com/glossary.php.

The Guide to the Other Side. http://www.askalana.com/os/otherside1.html.

The Power of Intention. http://lifetrainingonline.com/blog/the-power-of-intention-chapters-1-6.htm.

"The Pythagorean Theory of Music and Color." Internet Sacred Text Archive (ISTA). www.sacred-texts.com/eso/sta/sta19.htm.

Thompson, Vicky. "The Spiritual Meaning of Sin." http://www.journeywithspirit.com/christianspirituality_meaning_sin.htm.

Thornbury, Kendra E. "Vibration Revealed—3 Manifesting Need to Knows." http://ezinearticles.com/?Vibration-Revealed---3-Manifesting-Need-to-Knows&id=2420074.

Use Your Natural Talents: Power in the Power of Intention. http://practicalintention.com/?p=10.

"What is the Christ Consciousness?" http://www.ctrforchristcon.org/christ-consciousness.asp.

"What is a Light Worker?" http://lightworkers.org/what-is-a-lightworker-are-you-a-lightworker.

"When the Butterfly Effect Took Flight" http://www.technologyreview.com/article/422809/when-the-butterfly-effect-took-flight.

"Who Are Ascended Masters?" http://www.sanctuaryoflight.org/Worthy-Gleanings.html.

"Working with Angels and Spirit Guides." http://www.wingsforthespirit.com/working-with-angels-and-spirit-guides.htm.

Quotes:

http://blog.gaiam.com/quotes/authors/william-butler-yeats/40033
http://blog.gaiam.com/quotes/taxonomy/term/25530/0?page=30
http://thinkexist.com/quotes/Dan_Rather/
http://thinkexist.com/quotes/Dr_Martin_Luther_King_Jr/
http://thinkexist.com/quotes/Dr_Wayne_W_Dyer/
http://thinkexist.com/quotes/henry_david_thoreau/
http://thinkexist.com/quotes/john_muir/
http://thinkexist.com/quotes/Joseph_Addison/
http://thinkexist.com/quotes/Joseph_Campbell/
http://thinkexist.com/quotes/Mahatma_Gandhi/
http://thinkexist.com/quotes/Margaret_Mead/
http://thinkexist.com/quotes/Marianne_Williamson/
http://thinkexist.com/quotes/Marilyn_Ferguson/
http://thinkexist.com/quotes/michelangelo/
http://thinkexist.com/quotes/Neale_Donald_Walsch/
http://thinkexist.com/quotes/Paulo_Coelho/
http://thinkexist.com/quotes/Persian_Proverb/
http://thinkexist.com/quotes/Rumi/
http://thinkexist.com/quotes/Theilhard_de_Chardin/
http://thinkexist.com/quotes/William_Shakespeare/
http://thinkexist.com/quotes/Winston_Churchill/
http://thinkexist.com/quotes/Voltaire/
http://ivblog.wordpress.com/quotes/#DVirtue
http://lifecoachlakeway.com/general/your-true-nature/
http://www.askalana.com/blog/chanelling-nature-of-intention/
http://www.brainyquote.com/quotes/authors/k/khalil_gibran.html

http://www.entheos.com/quotes/by_teacher/Seng-ts'an
http://www.goodreads.com/quotes/620676-your-profession-is-not-what-brings-home-your-weekly-paycheck
http://www.iamthatiamministries.net/outpourings_of_st_germain_3.htm
http://www.mkgandhi.org/articles/discovery.htm
http://www.soundsofsirius.com/articles/our-father/

CDs/Audios/DVDs/Movies:

Kearns, Kell. *The Consciousness of the Christ: Reclaiming Jesus for a New Humanity.* Heaven on Earth Films, 2005.

Shadyac, Tom. *I Am, the Movie.* Flying Eye Productions in association with Homemade Canvas Production, February, 2011.

Williamson, Marianne. *Being in Light.* Hay House Publishing, March 1, 2003.

Williamson, Marianne. *Manifesting Abundance.* Hay House Publishing, April 1, 2004.

Made in the USA
San Bernardino, CA
22 December 2014